The Charm...

The Power of
Positive Choice!

By Gus Searcy

Published By TBS Marketing
18340 Yorba Linda Blvd. #107-445
Yorba Linda, CA 92886

The stories in this book are true. Some names have been changed or omitted to protect the privacy of them and that of their families.

ISBN# 978-0-9850185-0-4
Motivational / Autobiography

Library of Congress Control Number: 2012900298

For information about Special discounts for bulk purchases, please contact TBS Marketing attention Special Sales: thecharm@mail.com

Cover Designed By: Jericho Cordero

First Addition
1.01

Dedication:

**I dedicated this book to my mother:
Dorothy Lazar Searcy,
who demonstrated a love greater than
most children will ever know, men will
ever understand, and women will ever
have.**

Dotty

Meaning:
Gift of God

Origin:
 Greek

FOREWORD

By Pat Adeff

Every once in a great while – if you are very lucky – a person will enter your life who changes it forever. Mr. Gus Searcy is that person for me. Several years ago when I first met him, my initial response was "What a nice guy!" After spending a little more time with him, my opinion changed to "What an incredible human being!" Now my opinion is as follows: "Gus Searcy is a man who cares deeply for his fellow man. He truly wants what is best for others. He sees what few others see. He understands those things that most of us struggle to understand. He blesses many lives on a routine day-to-day basis."

One of the things Mr. Searcy accomplished was to help me understand my full potential and reach for star-high dreams. His mentoring has allowed me to live a larger life. His caring has given me the insight to care more deeply for others. His leadership has given me the training to make the small positive decisions, that lead to success. His outlook on life set a standard of courage for me to follow. This book will do the same for you, if you let it. If you want a better life, if you want to grow even more as a human being, read this book cover to cover. The lessons within will change your life for the better, forever.

* * * * *

Ms. Adeff's background is in the education field where she was a successful teacher, and then later became school principal of a leading private school in Orange County, California. Now that she has retired, she is an award-winning children's playwright, with many of her plays being produced in community theatres throughout Southern California.

The mindset of the author

For years, people have asked me to write a book and for years, I said no. After much coercion, I relented. I hope you will find some value from the stories herein.

Bad things happen to people all of the time. When that moment arrives, each of us makes a decision and chooses a path based upon the negative thing or event. Too often though, it is easier for us to take the negative stance rather than the positive one. We blame someone or something else for our lack of success. We take on the role of victim and buy into the "poor me" logic.

The purpose of the book is to try to get people understand there is always a positive choice in every bad situation and to look for, and make the positive choice they might not otherwise be willing to take. This book is a collection of true stories. It focuses on the point, that when a negative event happened, the positive choice or direction was made, the one most people would not have taken, with remarkable and life altering results. A web site documents many of those events or results from those events. It is **www.thecharm.info**

The ability for positive thinking is something we all are capable of doing and it is my hope this book will inspire you to make more positive choices in your life.

Gus Searcy

A note to the potential reader of this book

Spelling, Punctuation and Grammar: Much time, energy, and effort was put into the writing of this book. Even more time has been spent on the editing, changing and correcting it for accuracy, nearly three times as long in fact. Some readers get so caught up looking for mistakes when reading a new book they over look the message or idea the author was trying to convey. We have tried our best to make it as error free as possible. In fact, within the team of people that has been involved with this book, there have even been **"Pun**ctuati**on Wars'.** Therefore, before you proceed any further, I would like you to take a moment and read the following paragraph. If you successfully can, then you may want to proceed with the rest of book. If you can't, then that would be a good time to consider finding a different one!

Cna yuo raed tihs? Fi yuo cna raed tihs tehn yuo hvae a sgtrane mnid. Olny 55 plepoe out of 100 cna. i cdnuol't blveiee taht I cluod aulaclty uesdnatnrd waht i wsa rdanieg. The phaonmneal pweor of teh hmuan mind mekas it psoislbe. Aoccdrnig to rsceearh at Cmabrigde Uinervtisy, it dseno't mtaetr in waht oerdr the ltteres in a wrod are. Teh olny iproamtnt tihng is taht the frsit and lsat ltteer be in the rghit pclae. Teh rset can be a taotl mses and yuo cna sitll raed it whotuit a pboerlm. Tihs is bcuseae the huamn mnid deos not raed ervey lteter by istlef, but teh wrod as a wlohe. Azanmig rihgt? yaeh and i awlyas tghuhot slpeling was ipmorantt! I hvae awlsay bene a bda splleer and sepll cehck hsa awlyas falied me. So if yuo cna dael wtih a splelnig or garmemr erorr now and tehn, plaese cnotniue raednig and ejnoiyng this boko

Please don't let as small error in spelling, grammar or punctuation distract you from the positive lessons herein.

Table of Contents

Chapter 1

Dotty and the Charm

*"A Love greater than most
Children will ever know."*

Once upon a time, – a long time ago – in a land far, far
away called Los Angeles, California; there lived a man
and a woman. They loved each other very much and so,
were married. After several months of normal efforts
with no results, they went to the doctor to find out why
they had been unable to conceive a child. After many
tests, the doctor concluded they would never be able to
conceive. Despite this struggle and set back, and because

they loved each other even more now, they decided to stay together.

The years came and went and one day the wife became very ill. She asked her husband to take her to the doctor because she did not know what was wrong. At the doctor's office after they ran all the tests, it turned out she was not sick at all. In fact, she was pregnant. They were extremely excited about this. The husband was especially excited because he was known in the neighborhood as the *old man* and now he was the *stud*.

Everything was going quite well for the happy couple until their doctor's visit at the end of the first trimester. At their appointment, the doctor sat the couple down and informed them the wife had contracted lymphatic cancer. They had only two options available: The first choice was the wife could be treated for the cancer. With treatment, she would probably survive, but she would lose the baby. The second choice was she could carry the baby to term, but she would not be able to survive. Without hesitation, she (and accepting no discussion from her husband) chose the second option, to carry the baby and assuredly die.

Inherently she was an incredible mother. Her name was Dotty. Knowing now the certainty of her death, and knowing she was not going to be able to continue to raise her baby, Dotty, despite her declining health, went about the miraculous task of figuring it all out. Not only who would love and marry her husband when she died; but who would also love and raise their baby, as she would have if she had lived. The husband and wife had discussed their options in great depth before agreeing he would remarry. With this choice, there were two conditions.

Dotty's first condition was the baby was never to know the second wife (his stepmother) was not the biological mother. Dotty was not going to allow an extra opportunity for childhood rebellion, especially, with remarks like, "You're not my real mother."

The second condition was the husband was not to wait the traditional grieving period of one year before remarrying. Instead, he was to remarry as soon as possible because the baby needed a mother right away.

The delivery went well and the baby was born healthy. Six months later, Dotty died. Per Dotty's request, and their agreement, the father remarried a few short months after her death. The woman Dotty had selected was a widow who lost her husband a few years before.

Any relationship is challenging in so many ways. For many, the hardest part is finding someone to love who can love them back in a mutual and harmonious way. These two did not even find each other. Rather, the child's mother brought them together. Their job was to raise this child with care and love while protecting him from the truth. Not only did they do it; they grew to love each other more than they had imagined was even possible. In fact, they were the love of their lives. So much so even when they were in their mid 60's she would sit on his lap and they would watch TV together. What a miracle it was. The child was raised in a very happy household.

In this household, among other things, was a room, that contained a four-drawer filing cabinet. One day, when the child was about fourteen years old, his mother called to him and asked for some information from that very filing cabinet. When he was young, he was unable to see into the top drawer of the filing cabinet. As a man, he would look down upon the top of the filing cabinet. However, at the age of fourteen, he was just the right height to see all the way into the back of the top drawer of the cabinet.

When he went to put the information back, he saw in the back of the top drawer a tab said "Adoption." Since the cabinet had never been off limits, he decided to read the file. Consequently, he discovered he, in fact, had been adopted.

With such news, he did not know what to do or what to think. He called his best friend to come over. He too read the file and confirmed, indeed, he was adopted. At that point, his friend asked, 'What are you going to do about this?' The boy replied, "Absolutely nothing," as he put the file back in the filing cabinet and closed the drawer.

His friend asked why he was going to do nothing. The boy replied, "Well, it's very simple. I love my dad. I love my mom. They love me. Why mess it up?" And he did just that – he said nothing.

Several years came and went. A day came when his father was in intensive care. Thinking he was going to die (fortunately he did not die) his father kept saying, 'Take care of your mom, you don't know what she has been through for you . . . Take care of your mom, you don't know what she has been through for you.' Finally, the son said, "Hey. Don't worry about it. It's OK. I know. I was adopted."

His mother and father both looked at him and asked, 'how did you know?' He then told them about the filing cabinet. Astonished, they asked, 'Why haven't you said anything before now?' Then he replied, "Well, it's real simple. You love me. I love you. Why mess it up?" Then they said, "Okay but, you're being adopted is not exactly the whole story." That night when the mother and son came back to the house, they sat down and she told him the story about Dotty, his biological mother.

He did not say anything to her at that moment, but he did not believe the story one bit. Instead, he said to himself, "No way. The story is excessively farfetched to be true. They just made it up to make me feel better."

Some years later, after his father had died and his mother was in a nursing home, he decided to visit his Auntie

Jewel. Even though his whole life he had been taught to call her "*Auntie Jewel*," she was not really his aunt. At the time, she was in her late eighties and he was in his mid-twenties. Most twenty-five year olds do not spend a lot of time going to visit people in their late eighties. Nonetheless, for some reason he decided to go visit her.

During some point in their conversation, she interrupted him and said, 'Oh, you know about Dotty, don't you?' Dotty was Dorothy Lazar, the boy's biological mother. He replied, "Yes I do." She said, 'Wait here just a moment, I have something for you.' She rose from her chair, and went to her bedroom. Despite the fact she was in her late eighties and had probably moved many times throughout her life, she returned promptly with what she had been looking for and had a small box in her hand.

She sat down next to him on the couch and said, 'I have a story to tell you.' She then told him the exact same story his parents had told him about how he was adopted and who his birth mother really was. She said he had been adopted so if anything happened to his father he would still be cared for by the woman Dotty had selected to raise him. Then she added the following information, 'I was your real mother's best friend and it has been a joy watching you grow up. You are just like her in many ways. One, you are way too trusting and two, just like her, you go out of your way to help people. She would be very proud of you.' Just before she died, she said, 'When the time is right, give this to my baby, tell him I love him and will watch over him always.' Then Dotty removed a little sterling silver heart from her charm bracelet and gave it to me, 'I have been keeping it for you all of these years.'

Because Dotty made the choices she did, even though they were difficult to make, a chain of positive events was set in motion, that helped changed the world forever.

My name is Gus Searcy, while Hazel May Dunn Searcy was my *Mom* who raised me, (stepmother is not acceptable to me) Dotty was my biological mother. To this day, I wear that little silver heart charm on a chain around my neck and this is my life story.

Chapter 2
The Secret and Magic!

Thousands of times a day, we make choices. Many of those choices change our whole lives even though they seem insignificant at that moment. I live my life consciously making every choice I can as positive as possible. As easy as this is for me to do, it is equally as easy for me not to do. By simply choosing the most positive option, time and time again, I have opened a countless number of doors of opportunity for myself, almost as if, by magic!

When I was seven years old, the Boy Scouts of America and Disneyland did something quite remarkable. One day a year, they opened Disneyland early so the Boy Scouts could ride all the rides without having to wait in the long lines. This was a momentous event for me, especially because as long as I could remember this was the first time I was ever away from my parents. It was a memorable day for me indeed.

When the gates opened all the kids took off running – yes, I know we were supposed to walk. However, we all took off running. I ran as fast as I could around the corner, across the main park, down Main Street and all the way to Sleeping Beauty's Castle. When I arrived at the castle, I was a bit winded so I stopped to catch my breath. While I rested a moment, I began listening to the song that was playing, the song was *When You Wish Upon A Star,* and the lyrics went something like this:

When you wish upon a star
Makes no difference who you are
Anything your heart desires will come to you
If your heart is in your dreams
No request is too extreme
When you wish upon a star, your dreams come true.

I was only seven years old that day at Disneyland and I was already a little cynical. I thought to myself, well, if this were true, it would be like magic. It was in those exact moments, while I listened to those lyrics, I learned about **The Law of Attraction** for the very first time. The power of **The Secret** has allowed me to bring my dreams to reality repeatedly. The song became the theme song of my life. I listen to it almost every single day.

As I turned around to leave the castle, much to my surprise, there was a Magic Shop. It is not there today, but it was there then. I had never seen a magic shop before and it seemed like too much of a coincidence, I had just uttered to myself only a moment ago … "That would be like magic…," so I walked inside. As I stepped inside the magician said to me, 'Come here kid, watch this.' I was amazed by what he showed me. I spent almost all the money I had that day in the magic shop and became a 'closet magician.'

I practiced magic all the way through grammar school, junior high school, high school and even college. No one knew I did magic. I just practiced when I was alone in my room. Occasionally I would do something for my mom and dad. Every now and then, we would have company over and my dad would say, 'Hey, do the thing you did the other day.' However, I never performed in any public setting. I loved magic so much I did not want to find out I wasn't any good at it, so I kept it as my secret. It was probably my biggest secret and I kept it a secret for a very long time.

When I was 21 years old my father took my mother, my girlfriend and I to the Shrine Auditorium, in Downtown Los Angeles. That night they had a live stage show including a famous magician who had just flown in from Japan for his début in the United States. That night I did not know him. Today I am grateful and honored we are friends.

I watched the show with immense enthusiasm from the front row of the balcony through my high-powered binoculars my father had given me for my 16th birthday. When the show was over my dad said to me, 'You know son, as long as you have been interested in magic, it seems like it's something you should look into. You seem to care a lot about it.' A few minutes later, my father had a heart attack and died. Those were the last words my father ever spoke to me.

At this point, I had two choices about magic: First, because I was so close to my father and so devastated by his death, I could have chosen to never do magic again. Or second, I could choose to find out how good I really was. . . I chose the latter.

In researching all the magic clubs and societies, worldwide, I found out the hardest and most prestigious one to become a member of is The Magic Castle, in Hollywood, California. The reason it's so difficult to get into is because you have to pass a test of magic in front of a panel of master magicians. The 'trick' is, during the test you may not use any items purchased from a magic shop. No gimmicks, just pure 'magic!'

I did become a member of The Magic Castle and I went on to become one of the highest paid magicians in the 70s, appearing at Comedy & Magic Clubs, Trade Shows, on Cruise Ships and even Las Vegas. My son Sean is now learning from me the art of magic as well.

What if I had chosen differently? I will never know what would have been, had I made those choices differently. However, what I do know is because of the positive choices I did make, a set of events occur, which (as you will see later) helped change the world!

Chapter 3

The Bully

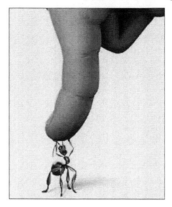

In Junior High School, I was a mild-mannered kid. I was very nice. I did not fight. Yet unfortunately, I was picked on quite a bit by bullies during those years. There was one bully in particular, Freddie Lork. Doesn't that even sound like a bully's name? He had it in for me big time. In the seventh grade, he was almost twice as tall as I was and was twice as strong as I was. In my mind, he was just a monster. He was so mean. He even had his own little Goon Squad. They would terrorize everyone.

Each day after gym class, we would all go back to the locker room to shower. Every day after his shower, Freddie Lork would walk by me and spit on me. I tried to do the right thing as we were taught to do; I told my dilemma to all of the P.E. teachers, however it did not matter. Every single day he would walk by and spit on me. It became such a routine I would not even bother getting dressed until he would walk by. This went on for quite a while.

One day I just snapped. I am not sure exactly what made this day so different from all the rest, but I decided even though I might die in the process; the abuse was going to end today. I had finally had enough. I had summoned the courage to face my fears. After my shower, I got a mouthful of water, went back to my locker, started to dress and mentally prepared for battle.

Note: The rows had been designed so there were lockers on both sides of the aisle and a bench down the middle. The bench had been cemented to the ground, so it could not be moved.

As we were all getting dressed, the two boys to either side of me, whom I was friends with, were just chitchatting away not noticing I was not talking. It wasn't too long before they realized I had a mouth full of water. As they realized the significance of what my mouth full of water meant, their eyes grew as big as saucers. The priceless look on their faces told you they knew they were about to witness an extraordinary event. They could not believe what I was about to do.

Sure enough, like every other day, Freddie came walking up the other side of the aisle just as he normally did.

Then, he spit on me, just as he normally did. However, this time I turned around and I spit back! Before he could do anything, I pushed him against the locker and when he bounced back, I spun him around and put him in a headlock. He went nuts! He tried with everything he could to kick me. Nevertheless, every time he would try to kick me he would hit the bench instead and his head would hit the locker. This made him even more furious. This kid was big and strong, but I had him in a really good headlock. I also knew if I let go, for so much as a moment, I was done for. All the kids began screaming.

Above the locker room was a mezzanine where the teachers had a birds-eye-view of the students. I finally looked up to see when one of the teachers was going to rescue me. Sure, enough all three teachers came out of their offices to see what all the commotion was. As one of the teachers headed for the stairs to come down another teacher grabbed his arm, stopped him. Now, I am not sure why he did, but my guess was he knew I pretty much had it under control for the moment and they were going to let Freddie squirm for a while. The teachers all knew what a menace he was.

All the while, Freddie was screaming terrible things. Freddie kept screaming things like, he was going to kill me and I was going to die. However, every time he tried to kick me, he would kick the bench instead and slam his head against the locker. After a couple of times, you would have thought he would have caught on, but he just kept at it. Clearly, he was not thinking straight. This went on for what felt like forever to me, until the teachers finally came down.

It took two teachers to pull him away from me. Fortunately, all of the kids told the teachers this had been going on every day. So, I was not in trouble.

This all happened during third or fourth period, right after lunch. It did not take long for the rumors to spread like wild fire, after school Freddie was going to kill me. Keep in mind, this guy could very easily carryout those words. He was truly a scary person.

The bell rang and school was out for the day. My classroom happened to be the classroom closest to the bike rack. The gym was probably 400 yards away. All the kids rushed out of their classrooms in anticipation to see what was going to happen next. Freddie Lork came tearing across the field after me as I jumped on my 10-speed bike as fast as I could, thinking to myself, "I am going to die." By the time, Freddie had arrived at the bike rack I had already gotten a bit of a head start. He jumped on someone's Stingray (a little one-speed bike) from the bike rack and rode after me.

At this point, I knew I would be ok. You see, just a few weeks before all this happened I had been sent to the principal's office for a speeding ticket for going 34 M.P.H. in a 25 M.P.H. zone. Yes, on my bicycle!

Sure enough, he never caught me and I made it home safe. Thankfully, he did not know where my house was. The next day though, I was afraid to return to school.

I never heard the full story, but apparently, that night Freddie and his Goon Squad were so upset about what had happened, they went out to stir up trouble. I'm not sure of what their rampage consisted of, but they wound up being arrested. Freddie ended up in Juvenile Hall and was never seen or heard from again.

I learned that day nobody should push you around. 'A bully' could be anyone or anything, a boss, a colleague, or even a company or organization. I learned you do not have to let anyone bully you. Even if they are bigger, badder, or stronger than you are, you can still triumph.

When I went to college, I had a bully of another breed to deal with. Fortunately, the lessons I had learned and the strength I gained from dealing with Freddie Lork made me a strong enough person to not let someone else hold me down.

While in college, I was on the college water polo team and I joined a fraternity, Sigma Alpha Epsilon. It turned out my water polo coach not only attended the college himself for his undergraduate work, but he had tried to join the same fraternity. Unfortunately, they did not accept him; he was not able to join S.A.E. He was less than pleased by my participation with this particular fraternity and he constantly gave me a hard time about it.

As the polo season progressed, his remarks escalated and persisted.

I played the second string goalie on our team. During one game toward the end of the season, the goalie in the pool was having an extremely rough day. We were down something like 0 to 8. In my opinion, any other coach would have replaced him. Everything the goalie could do wrong he had done.

With about 4 minutes left in the game, the coach walked up to me and said, 'Would you like to get in the game?' I said, "Sure, of course." With a terrible look of distain upon his face, he snipped back at me, 'Well, you're not going to. Go to the showers.' Obediently, I complied and headed to the showers.

No sooner had the door closed behind me and I could no longer see or hear what was happening, our goalie was thrown out of the game, naturally, at that point; in a game, the other goalie would take over and get in the pool. Since I was in the showers and out of earshot, the coach looked around and proceeded to ask the team, 'Where is Gus?'

Of course "abandoning your team" is not exactly a move that will earn you points with your teammates. After the game, the coach called a team meeting (That I was not invited to). After the coach spoke, my teammates voted me off the team without even hearing my side of the story.

This was extremely unfair and unjust. I decided the coach was clearly a bully and I was not going to stand for this. Therein lies the question. How do you get back at the coach for his unruly behavior without hurting the team?

After weighing a few options and evaluating the variables, I came up with the perfect solution. I called a meeting of my fraternity brothers and the girls from the local sorority. We planned an all out recruiting assault on the water polo team. By enlisting the help of those girls and with the help of their flirtatious influence, it was a great success.

Next year came and I was again on the water polo team. The difference was, this year, the entire first and second strings of the water polo team had all joined my fraternity, S.A.E. The coach could not exactly be mean to all of us.

The injustice was corrected and the team did not suffer in the process.

After the triumphant day in Junior High School with Freddie Lork, I adopted the following affirmation and it has carried me through many seemingly hopeless situations and encounters, including the struggles with my college water polo coach. Throughout my life, I have encountered bullies in other forms but from the two experiences I just shared, I was ready for them. Now I live my life by the following quote:

"Though I have fears, I will learn to face them and use them as stepping stones towards success."

It is my hope you too can harness the power to face your fears and turn them into stepping stones toward success so you too may be triumphant against injustice.

Chapter 4

$1.10 to Six Figure Stocks

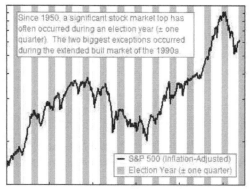

Since 1950, a significant stock market top has often occurred during an election year (± one quarter). The two biggest exceptions occurred during the extended bull market of the 1990s

— S&P 500 (Inflation-Adjusted)
■ Election Year (± one quarter)

I have always had an affinity for numbers. I was very good at math. I am in the 98th or 99th percentile in the math section for both the SAT and ACT tests. I came prewired mathematically inclined and I love numbers.

When I was growing up we had a newspaper delivered, it was called the **Herald Examiner**. Every morning when the paper would come, my dad would get it first. He would take out the Sports section. Then my mom would take out the Coupon section. Finally, I would get it and go straight for the Comic section. After we each had removed the section we were most interested in, there was always one section left that would beckon my attention. At the very back of the newspaper, there were pages and pages of numbers.

One day at the age of about fifteen, I finally asked my dad, "What are all these numbers?" He said, 'It is something called the Stock Market. You can make money in it.' I replied, "Oh really?" This intrigued me, so I began to learn about it. Diligently, I started learning all about how the stock market worked, including doing all my own research. I studied Price Earnings Ratios, Marginal Propensity to Change, Margin calls, grafting, charting, trends and all kinds of related things.

Keep in mind, with computers and technology today the research, which had taken me weeks back then, would literally only take seconds now. Back then, you had to order special little books in the mail and chart out the history of each individual stock; there was a whole process. Now you can simply look up all of those facts and charts on-line in seconds.

After all my studying, charting and research I came up with what I thought was a workable system. I used the American Stock Exchange instead of the New York Stock Exchange because it was more volatile. The added volatility (daily price fluctuations) and new companies gave me the environment I was looking for. With my system, I was able to be wrong half the time and still actually make money. One of the key elements to this system was my lack of emotional attachment to the money. To maintain an emotional disconnect with the money from the moment I spent the money to purchase the stock I considered the money spent and gone. That way if I ever did actually "lose" any money, it did not feel like I was losing money, because the money was already gone.

After all my research and becoming quite comfortable and confident with my system I started sharing my excitement and predictions with my dad. I'd say, "Hey Dad! Look! Look! Watch this stock is going to go up." He would reply, 'Sure son. Sure.' Then I would come back to him a few weeks later, "Look! Look Dad! It went up! Just like I said it would!" Well, this went on for a little while.

Finally, my dad took me to an event. This event or meeting was similar to a "business opportunity meeting" you see these days. This event was held by a stockbrokerage company and was designed to inform people about the stock market, to encourage them to invest in stocks.

After the presentation was over, my dad walked me up to the broker who was putting on the presentation and said, "My son wants to play the stock market. He keeps telling me all this stuff and I have no idea what he is talking about. Nor do I know if *HE* has any idea of what he is talking about. Would you please speak with him for a few minutes and find out if he really knows what he is saying?

The broker turned to me and asked me how I picked a stock. I took out all my charts, showed him my research and everything else I had been using. My dad looked at him and said, 'So…?' The broker replied, 'Not only does your son know what he is talking about, but I am pretty sure he knows more than I do.'

After that, my dad caved. He signed the Power of Attorney over to me as an adult so I could play the stock market at age 16. The condition was I had to use my own money. So, I went out and obtained my first job at McDonald's. I worked my way up to making $1.10 per hour and used the money to buy stock. Soon after playing the stock market it was spread around the school I was good at it. The teachers began coming to me and asking me for stock advice. In addition, as a sophomore I was actually lecturing in the senior's Economics classes on "How to Play the Stock Market."

On our lunch breaks, when everyone would go hang out, I would run to the payphone to call my Stockbroker to find out how my stocks were doing. Eventually, the teachers began following me to the payphone and took notes.

During Christmas Break, while everyone else was off goofing around, I would take a bus from Downey, California to Downtown Los Angeles, everyday, and I would sit at the Pacific Coast Stock Exchange and watch the numbers go by. To this day, I still occasionally invest in the stock market. I still understand all the philosophies, principals, and complexities I had learned years before. However, I cannot seem to play, these days, without the emotional attachment. It was so much easier then to be unattached and without serious responsibilities or financial obligations. If I lost all the money, I would still have had a roof over my head and plenty of food. As an adult, it is a little different situation.

The money I earned from playing the stock market, in my early years of high school, later helped pay for a 7-Eleven store, my condominium and cash for my first car. The magic here is it all started from those newspapers lying on the floor every Sunday, with all those numbers on them staring at me. I was curious and did the due diligence to learn about it. What unfolded from those pages of numbers was truly extraordinary.

Sometimes the "positive choice" is doing something more than just noticing something. It is knowing how to look for the opportunity as well. I had 'noticed' those pages on the floor for many Sundays before I chose to even inquire about them, let alone pursue the possibilities and opportunity they held.

One of my favorite stories, which truly illustrates this point, goes like this: There once was a shoe company, who sent a salesperson to Africa to check on the potential for its products there. A few days after going into the bush, the company's salesperson reported, *'I'm coming home. There is no market here. Nobody wears shoes.'* The company then decided to send its top salesperson to the exact same location. Within a matter of hours, the second salesperson enthusiastically reported his findings to the company. *'The market is ripe here. There are fantastic opportunities. Nobody owns shoes yet!'*

The major difference between the two salespeople was one had a positive attitude!

Chapter 5

Beer Raffle

As mentioned earlier I had been in a fraternity in college, S.A.E. (Sigma Alpha Epsilon) because I went to a commuter college most of the students in our fraternity were much older than me. My being only eighteen and most of them were at least twenty-one years old. Since I was the youngest, newest and only freshman brother in the house, my thoughts and suggestions were generally ignored.

One evening at our fraternity meeting, it was mentioned we needed to raise some money to pay for our upcoming parties. One of the guys suggested we do a 'Beer Raffle.' I looked at the person sitting next to me and asked, "What's a Beer Raffle?" He answered, 'Well, we buy a case of beer and we raffle it off for fifty cents a ticket.' This confused me so I asked, "Why are we doing this exactly?" He replied, 'To make money.' I was still confused so I asked, "Well, how much money can we make doing that?" He said we could make a few hundred dollars, about enough to throw a party. Now, from my stock market experience, earning a few hundred bucks to throw a party was nothing to write home about.

So I said, "If we really want to make money, I know how to make money. Why don't we have a really big raffle where we raffle off huge prizes and makes lots and lots of money?" They basically said, 'Hey, that's nice and all, but no one is going to give us all of the stuff we would need.' They laughed me out of the meeting.

One should know better than to laugh me out of a meeting. They had laid down the gauntlet and it was all the challenge I needed. After much thought, I put together a little "plan of attack," if you will. One key thing I learned about business, along the way is, no matter how good business is, business is always bad. No matter when it is, back when I was in college or right now, it is always the same. No matter how good business is, it is always bad, especially when it comes to donating money, or prizes.

Learning and understanding that principal was important. Companies are not usually willing to do donate unless it is something extremely significant or emotional to them personally. However, they will all spend money on advertising. With this basic business knowledge, I went out into our community that week on a mission, to find the grand prize.

The following week, at our fraternity meeting I began the meeting, "I suggest instead of having a Beer Raffle we do something on a much larger scale and call it the "Sigma Alpha Epsilon Summer Sweepstakes." We will give away all kinds of prizes and the grand prize will be a brand new Suzuki motorcycle worth about two thousand dollars." Then I stood up, and I had a full-sized poster of the motorcycle all rolled up with weights on the bottom so when I let go it unrolled like a scroll. Then I said, "And this is the Grand Prize and I already have it donated 100% for free."

They were completely shocked. Then they asked me how much money this was all going to cost. I told them all I would need was a budget of about $300 and 30 days to finish preparing. After asking again if I had really landed the motorcycle as a grand prize, they told me to go ahead with my Summer Sweepstakes plan.

Since I had a motorcycle of my own, what I did was to go around to all the local motorcycle shops and spoke to their advertising department. Knowing the cost of a half-page ad at my university's newspaper and having researched what adds in the local papers were costing, I knew the kind of money these companies were spending on advertising. What I had learned, that they did not know was the fact that the same ad for my fraternity, a non-profit organization, in the same newspaper was about $1/20^{th}$ of the price they would pay. I offered them a half-page ad in that same paper for the entire contest period, plus the exclusive privilege of having a booth on campus between the library and cafeteria, where all the students walked by every day and placing their motorcycle in the booth. Additionally we would "man" the booth and have someone there to hand out brochures about their motorcycle and store; they could also be there physically to draw the winning ticket at the end of the raffle.

I put this proposal together in a little presentation folder and went around to all of the local businesses. Aside from the Suzuki motor cycle as the grand prize, I ended up getting a gas-powered mini-bike, a 10-speed bicycle, two tennis rackets and a few other things.

In the midst of it all, I was actually in a motorcycle accident and ended up in the hospital for a time. While I was in the hospital, my fraternity brothers took my presentation folder and told me not to worry, they could take care of the rest. Apparently, they still had not learned how to think bigger because all they could get from the local businesses they went to was one bottle of wine and a little camera.

With the Summer Sweepstakes, we ended up earning about several thousands of dollars all in about 30 days.

So at the next fraternity meeting after the sweepstakes I brought up the fact we had wanted a fraternity house. I told them I knew how we could make $250,000 in one night. I went on to give them the details of how it would be more than possible.

I had already contacted the Forum Arena in Inglewood, California and tentatively reserved it. It was dependent on them receiving our $6,000 deposit by the following week. I had already spoken to the agents for the bands

Deep Purple, The Carpenters, and the headliner, Neil Diamond. Neil Diamond was only going to cost $40,000 for the night. Remember this was 1971.

We were going to do a charity concert. I informed them I had already spoken to the Children's Hospital in Los Angles and they had already agreed to put their name on the event as the charity. I also had the marketing department from KHJ a well-known local radio station willing to promote the event. One hundred percent of the proceeds were going to go to charity. The Children's Hospital was going to receive over half of the proceeds and our fraternity was going to receive the rest, remember, we were also a non-profit organization. I had already figured out the necessary math. The tickets were only going to cost $18 each and after everyone else had been paid, we were going to make a total of about $250,000 in one night! I let them know all I needed was for them to vote yes and let me go ahead.

They were so afraid and unwilling to expand their realm of thinking to believe this was even possible, they actually said 'no' and did not agree to let me go through with it.

* * *

One of my colleague's favorite books is written by Dr. David J. Schwartz and titled, "The Magic of Thinking Big." He liked it so much he gave me a copy. The story I just shared with you is a perfect example of how much the average individual passes up simply because he or she is not willing to think big enough. It is truly tragic. My hope is this story inspires you to think BIGGER, even if it's just a little bigger.

Chapter 6

Condo vs. Car

At the age of 19, I had acquired quite a bit of cash in the bank. At the same time, I did not have many bills. That year a new car came onto the market called a Bricklin. It was a very fancy, gull-winged sports car. It was quite expensive, but because I had the money, I decided I was going to buy one. I was going to be one of the first people to own one. I believe I had reserved number 32 off the assembly line. The car was manufactured in Canada. My plan was to fly out to Chicago (where it was to be delivered) during the summer when school was out, and drive it home.

Before it was time to go pick up the car, a very beautiful young woman from college invited me to go snow skiing with her and her friends. She was cute, I had never been snow skiing before, and I decided it would be fun, so the decision was made to go. Since I had never skied before, I did not have any ski equipment and told her we should go shopping so she could pick out the best of everything needed for the trip and I would buy it. Actually to this day most of it is still in my possession.

Off we went to a place called Mammoth Mountain. I had never been there before. From being on the water polo team, I was very athletic, so it was no problem catching on to skiing. We skied all day and had a wonderful time.

The next morning I woke up earlier than everyone else and I sat down to read the paper and something in the paper caught my eye. When everyone was dressed and ready to go skiing for the day I informed them I would not be skiing with them, instead I was going to stay behind.

When they came home that night from skiing, they had dirt, mud, and ice all over their boots. As they started to walk into the condo with their dirty boots, I looked at them and said, "Hey. What are you doing? Don't come in here with those dirty boots you are going to get this place all dirty. Leave the boots outside." They looked at me a bit perplexed and said jokingly, 'What? Do you own the place or something?' And I said, "Yes. I do."

Earlier in the morning, while reading the paper, I had noticed there was a for sale ad for the very condominium we were staying in, Chamonix Unit #59. Since I really enjoyed the town and the complex, when they went off skiing for the day, I decided to go find out more information about it. What I found out was, for less money than I was going to have to put down for the Bricklin car that I was so excited about, I could buy the condominium instead. The condominium was an asset, that would increase in value while the Bricklin was a liability, which would decrease in value. While I wanted the car very much I decided the condominium would be a more intelligent decision. Despite the fact I was nineteen years old, I understood the value of accumulating assets.

* * *

When I attended my first 'Home Owners Meeting', I learned most of the other owners were lawyers, doctors, dentists and people of similar stature. When I arrived at the meeting, the people at the door laughed a little, and then one said, 'I'm sorry but this meeting is only for the home owners.' At which time I replied, "I am one of the home owners!" After the initial shock wore off, we started sharing stories. I let them know I was planning to rent it out and they all had advice of one kind or another to offer me. They were all very clear and persistent I should not put anything in the condominium I liked or was of any value because it was guaranteed someone would steal it.

Maybe I was just naive, but I did not believe them. Instead of heeding their warning, I went out and bought the best things I could find to put in to the condominium. I bought crystal stemware, the largest color TV on the market at the time, one of the very first microwave ovens and books galore. The place was absolutely beautiful.

While all the other condo owners warned me it was a bad idea and all of my nice things were going to be stolen, my condominium became one of the most rented condos in Mammoth. What made my condo so unique and desirable was because I had upgraded it with those nice things.

A woman from a company, then called, T.R.W. knew me and heard I had a condominium in Mammoth for rent. She rented it from me. She was so impressed by how beautifully appointed and furnished it was compared to all of the other condos they had rented there on previous vacations. She started telling all her friends about it and actually put up a sign on their bulletin board for me. Suddenly all these people from T.R.W. started renting it, and the word spread. It was practically booked solid all year round. I hardly went there myself since there was always a waiting list to rent it.

Because I had decorated it so well, it truly felt like a home and renters treated it as such. In all the years I rented the condo, not once was anything removed that was not supposed to be, except for one paperback book. My guess is someone took the book home accidentally. I truly doubt it had been stolen. In addition, nothing in the condo was ever broken.

I owned the condominium for many years until I traded it for a home in Cypress, California, which I still own today. The home has increased a great deal in value over the years since I acquired it. In the property trade, I truly made the better deal. If I sold the house today, I could buy three condominiums in Mammoth. Additionally, it turns out I could still buy the car today for one half the amount I was going to pay for it back then. In addition, I have made more than 50 times the amount on the condominium and home because of that positive choice.

One of the temptations younger people have is to spend money instead of investing it. If they spent just a little time on investing, they would find they could still have the fun they are looking for. Owning a condo at age, nineteen, was not exactly a depressing situation.

Note: As of today, the Bricklin is worth about $6,000 while the condominium purchase was parlayed into over a $600,000 asset.

Robert Kiyosaki in his book **Rich Dad Poor Dad** teaches the value of creating assets, which spin off cash as opposed to acquiring more liabilities, that is what most people do. It appears I may have been wired at birth with a great deal of "Personal Development" and "Wealth Principles." This story is one of those examples.

Chapter 7

Flunked to Success

"Experience, you can't get it until you've got it, and no one will give it to you to get it."

-Gus Searcy

All through high school and college, I played on the school's water polo team. One of the fringe benefits of being on a sports team was you had first pick for your classes because you had to coordinate your class schedule with your travel schedule. The benefit alone made the suffering one had to endure during practice, worthwhile. As a junior in college, one of the required courses for my business degree was a Beginning Computer Programming Class. At the time, the only available class, which fit into my schedule, was a night class. Keep in mind back then computers were the size of buildings. It was FORTRAN, COBOL and Punch Cards. So there I was, having just turned twenty-one and in this evening computer programming class.

I remember every detail from my first night of class as if it had happened yesterday. The door was at the back of the classroom. The class was scheduled to begin at 7:00 p.m. At 7:05 p.m., there was no teacher. At about 7:10 p.m. a man blew into the room in a rumpled grey suit with a red burgundy briefcase. He went up to the front of the room, tossed his briefcase across the table and said,

'Sorry guys, I actually work for a living. I am sorry I am late. Let me tell you how the class is going to work. I grade on a straight curve. Someone in here is going to get an **A** and someone in here is going to get an **F**. The next thing you need to know is we are not going to mess around; we are going to work at the speed of the class. However fast the class goes, this is how fast we are going to go. By the way, how many people in here do programming during the day, for a living?'

Everyone in the class raised their hand, except me. Remember, this was a "beginning class." However, these were all professional programmers during the day. In fairness to them, this class was required for their business degree, so they were taking it to meet that requirement.

So, it would be like someone who was fluent in Spanish taking a Spanish 101 class.

By the end of the second week of class, I "volunteered" for that **F**. I was so far behind I did not have a chance. Realizing now the gravity and reality, I was going to be getting an F in this class I thought to myself, "Wow! This is not good." What was I to do? Was I supposed to drop out of college? It was clear to me, there was no way I was ever going to be able to pass this class – I mean ever. It was so far beyond any level of interest or enthusiasm for me.

(Ironically, however, I was later offered an associate professor position to teach the Advanced Computer Programming Class at the very same college. However, that's another story all in itself.)

A couple of days after I "volunteered" for the **F** (the computer class that I did end up flunking); I was in my Economics class listening to my professor lecture about the Laws of Supply and Demand. I had heard the Laws of Supply and Demand a hundred times before, but this time I began to free associate while I listened. I thought to myself, next year if I somehow manage to pass the computer programming class, I will graduate on the same day as about 900 people will graduate from my college with grades equal to or better than mine. Additionally in the Los Angeles area, California and in fact, in the entire United States of America, I figured approximately 2.3 million people were going to graduate college at about the same time I was, with grades equal to or better than mine.

The question then became, 'Why should someone hire me over anyone of them?' The answer: 'Not a reason in the world!' The next question was then, 'What would make me more marketable?' Answer: 'Experience!' Herein lays the *Catch 22*. You can't get it until you've got it, and no one will give it to you to get it. I thought to myself, well, there must be a solution; I wonder what it will be. (As I began to try to find solutions to this predicament, my thoughts were sent out to the universe and *The Law of Attraction* began to work.)

Later in the evening, when riding my motorcycle home from college, I passed the same empty corner lot I had passed hundreds of times before. This lot had been empty for years. That night something was different. There was a sign in the lot, and it said, "Coming Soon 7-Eleven. Own your own franchise." Now this sounded interesting.

Keep in mind, on my way to school that very same morning, I had passed the same empty corner lot, and there had not been a sign there. Coincidently, after I had used *The Law of Attraction* to ask for a solution, the very same day, the sign was there, and I saw it.

I did some research and found when you buy a 7-Eleven store you are essentially purchasing a management position. 7-Eleven decides the product pricing, and what inventory will be sold in the store. They do the payroll, the bookkeeping and the accounting. All you have to do is hire and fire employees, control the inventory levels (so you do not have too much of anything on hand), collect the money and deposit it into the bank. They do everything else. So I thought to myself; this sounds like experience, exactly the thing I need to make me more marketable.

I set up a meeting with South Land Corporation and informed them I wanted to own a 7-Eleven franchise. They said to me, 'You can't have it.' I said, "Why not?" They said, 'you do not meet our criteria.' So I asked, "What was the criteria?" They then informed me, 'The average 7-Eleven owner they were looking for was 35 years old, married with two children. You are only twenty-one.' I responded, "Oh, so you are *discriminating based on my age?*" Now at this time in the 70's discrimination was quite the hot topic. So they quickly replied, 'Oh, no no no. We are not doing that, however, it is "x" amount of money for the franchise.' So I pulled out my checkbook and started writing the check. They stopped me and said, 'What are you doing?' I said, "I'm writing you a check." They said, 'You can't write a check for that much! That's illegal!' I asked, "Why would it be illegal? The check is good." They were dumbfounded as they replied, 'How can it be good? How can you have so much money?' I replied, "Well, I have been playing the stock market since I was sixteen years old. There are also some neighbors who believe in me and will help financially back me. Why? Is there an issue here?"

What else could they do? They took the money and I became the youngest owner of a 7-Eleven franchise in the world.

* * *

Now, why did I do all this? Experience!
Knowing 90% of all businesses fail in their first year, my goal was to last one year.

One year later, there I was the youngest owner of a 7-Eleven franchise in the world and I thought to myself, "OK. This is good. But where will I be in ten years? ... The owner of a 7-Eleven franchise." This could be bad! Especially since as a 7-Eleven franchise owner you can have all the free Slurpees you want, and I was getting my money's worth. I had already gained twenty pounds. I figured ten more years and I could be about 300 pounds. This would definitely not be good.

I decided it was about time to see how well all of the experience had paid off. I started searching the ads for available positions and found a Fortune 500 company called SCM Corporation, which was advertising for a marketing assistant. I applied for the job, along with eighty other applicants and I was the youngest applicant by about four years.

I made it down to the final five finalists for the position, at that time they said to us, 'We will let you know by next Thursday.'

Wednesday came; the day before they were going to let us know. I woke up in the morning, dressed up in my suit and tie, walked into the office and asked to speak to the branch manager.

When the manager came out, I asked if I could speak to him for just a moment. He said, 'Sure. Come on in.' I went in, sat down, and said the following: "Now I know you are going to be making your decision tomorrow. I know eighty people applied for the position. I also know I made it down to the final five. No matter what happens, I would just like to know, for my own knowledge, how I made it to the final five."

He said, 'Well, we were very impressed by you. Most kids your age are out there goofing around and partying while you own your own business. You have demonstrated a great deal of initiative and enthusiasm. You seem to have many of the qualities we look for when we hire someone for our company.'

Then I responded, "Gee, that's great. I know you were going to decide tomorrow, but I am here right now. Why don't you just decide right now, and hire me?" He said, 'Well, that would not be very fair to the other four people.' At which time I looked to my left. I looked to my right. I looked at him and said, "So why aren't they here?" He replied, 'You know what? That is a good point.' And he hired me on the spot.

I went on to be one of the top salespeople at the company.

* * *

Too often, in life when someone encounters a small failure, (flunking a class; for example) they convince themselves they are losers and failures. They dwell on the negative of the situation without so much as considering a positive solution, let alone seeking one out. I did not do anything of that nature. I simply evaluated the situation for what it was and went about searching for a positive choice solution.

Chapter 8
Reasonable!

rea·son·able *adj* \\'rēz-nə-bəl, 'rē-z°n-ə-bəl\\
a: not extreme or excessive <reasonable requests>
b: <u>rational thinking</u> <be reasonable>
c: moderate, fair <a reasonable price>

As I thought and later confirmed from my 7-Eleven experience, setting yourself apart from the pack can make all the difference in life and in business.

If you were to meet me in person or speak to me on the phone, you might say something like: "Hi, how are you today?" You, as most people, would expect me to respond with something such as "Fine, thank you", "Great", "Excellent", "Wonderful," or some other such uplifting remark. We have been taught, regardless of how we really feel; we should always come across as upbeat and positive. While on the surface this is a good idea, it has become so anticipated and even expected, as a social mores, the response has lost its significance and therefore its power. So, if you were to greet me with: 'How are you today?' my response to you would be "Reasonable." I won many trips to the Super Bowl as one of the company's top salespeople. "Reasonable" is what got me there.

When I was hired on with SCM Corporation, I found my job was selling very expensive copy machines. To sell these machines you needed to make contact and get an appointment with the decision maker of the company. Due to the high cost of the copy machines, they were considered a capital expenditure and only the owner, president, CEO, or CFO could make such a decision. I later also found these are the same people who made other major company decisions as well, like employee benefit programs. Needless to say, getting to these people was extremely difficult. The companies' receptionists, secretaries, and purchasing departments are trained *gatekeepers* to keep you away from these decision makers. Most of the time when contacting a company you would be rerouted to someone who would tell you they handled this area of responsibility and they were not interested. Nine times out of ten, they were not the correct person, and could not have said 'yes' if their lives depended upon it, but many salespeople would accept the answer and suspend their sales efforts. This is when I learned a most important lesson: ***Never take "no" from someone who cannot say "yes!"***

The second lesson I had to learn was how to get past the gatekeeper. This turned out to be much easier then I had anticipated. Sales people tend to wine and dine their clients, that are usually the decision makers of the company. The secretaries and receptionists, in general, are over looked when it comes to the salesperson's attention and expense account. Given these gatekeepers truly did hold the keys to the company decision makers, it made sense to me to spend most of my time, when trying to get a new account, focusing my attention and expense account on them. I treated them as if they were the most important person in the company (and to me they were). It did not take long before it started to pay off. Soon, my phone was ringing every time their company's current copy machine broke down with a message from the receptionist or secretary, today was a good day to call and I should speak to Mr. or Ms. 'Decision Maker.' Armed with the knowledge the company's copy machine was broken and therefore productivity was being lost, I would place my first call to the decision maker.

This first contact was most important and in most cases, you only have, literally, seconds to make an impact and connection with the person on the other end of the phone. I quickly found the traditional "I'm great" had little impact or response. I needed to find a way, within six to eight seconds, which would show me the best way to deal with the person on the other end of the phone. As it turned out, the answer was going to be a combination of deep routed psychology, social mores, and split second timing. I could probably dedicate a whole book to this topic alone, but for the purposes of expediency, I will distill it down to the key elements.

First off, if you are not familiar with the term *Social Mores,* it is defined as, *"The accepted traditional customs and usages of a particular social group."* For example, when you are at the store and someone bumps into you by mistake you expect him or her to say, "Excuse me" or "I'm sorry." In turn, you are expected to say "its ok" or "No problem." Understanding this principal will be the key to the process.

The third lesson was to figure out how to set myself apart from all of the other sales people and calls these decision makers received every day. For me personally, when it comes to business, I do much better when I am dealing with the potential client on a personal level. This is true for most successful business people. Every company throughout the world knows the value of taking their clients out to eat. Additionally most men know the first date with a woman is to take her out somewhere to eat. However, very few people know exactly how and why this works or why it is so important.

The answer is Commensality: *"Fellowship at table; the act or practice of eating at the same table."* While this may seem obvious, it goes much deeper than this. Eating (feeding) is a primal act, and for centuries was only done in a safe place. During this feeding time, your guard was down, and you were most vulnerable, so it was only done with people you could trust implicitly. In modern society, *social mores* force us into situations where we are expected to eat with people we do not know. While conscientiously, we know when we are eating, a dinosaur or the cave man in the next cave is not going to come and eat us or take our food, yet we still, deep inside, harbor cautiousness when we eat. So when a man takes a date to dinner or a sales person takes a client to lunch, each side is forced to eat with the other and in the process the barriers are dropped and a bond of trust starts to form. If you can get your client to trust you, then they will more likely buy from you.

Knowing all of this of course did not solve my initial problem of getting on a personal level with my first contact of a new prospect and with only seconds to make it happen. You see, psychologically speaking, there are two types of people, *persons* and *nonpersons*. An example of a nonperson is someone who cuts you off on the freeway. You honk your horn, maybe cuss at them and if the cruise control button on the steering column of your car were a Proton Blaster instead, they would probably be history. You see, you do not perceive them as a real person. On the other hand if you were in line at the theater and someone were to cut in front of you, you would first take a more tactful approach and say something like "Excuse me; the line starts back there", before you start reaching for the Proton Blaster. This is because you see the person in front of you as real and therefore respond differently than you would in the car scenario.

When you make first contact with someone, you are a nonperson. The quicker you can get them to acknowledge you as a person, the greater your chances for success. There had to be a fast way to accomplish this change.

Over time and with much frustration, trial, and error I found an answer, that worked for me, and still does to this day. It goes like this:

When I make my first contact on the phone with a decision maker, I say, "Hello. Am I catching you at a good moment?" Decision makers are busy most of the time, and sometimes they are just swamped. For example, they may have a meeting in their office with people in front of them or they are running late to their next appointment and talking to me would make them even later. If they say it's not a good time I immediately say, "Thank you, I will try you back again." Then without further discussion, I hang up the phone. Notice, I did not say who I was or what I was calling about. Getting off the phone quickly shows the other person I am conscientious of their time and they are appreciative of it. I know this is true because the next time I call back they usually let me proceed. If when I first get them on the phone and they say 'yes this is a good time,' I say, "My name is Gus Searcy, how are you today?" There are several responses they can come back with, each will tell you something specific about the person you are talking to and what you should say next. When I said to them: "How are you today?" I offered up a question, which under common politeness and social mores demands a response. If their response is something like 'What can I do for you?' then they have willfully chosen to ignore the social more. They are strictly business and not wanting or allowing for a social interaction. In this case, my response is direct, to the point, and very businesslike (I am still a nonperson).

In the next scenario, I say, "My name is Gus Searcy, how are you today?" If they respond with something in the order of 'Fine, thank you.' they have acknowledged the greeting. However, they ignored the dictated social mores response of returning the greeting, with something like, 'and you?' This could mean they are simply overwhelmed or on a tight schedule at the moment. In this case my response is a little less direct, a little more informational, but still businesslike (again, I am still a nonperson).

In this next possibility, I say, "My name is Gus Searcy, how are you today?" This time their response might be 'Fine, thank you, and you?' Here, they have not only acknowledged my greeting they have taken the time to returne it to me as well. At this point, I say, **"Reasonable!"** This is not the expected response. It also is not a trite or impolite response. It's not flippant or disrespectful, but it is definitely different, unique, and unanticipated. If they do not respond to the remark, I understand that although they took the time to acknowledge my greeting and even return it, they were consciously keeping things on a business level and not allowing for small talk to enter the conversation. I therefore adjust my next few statements accordingly. (And I am still a nonperson). I will tell you, this is rare. The response *"Reasonable,"* is so different and unexpected, it usually elicits a response.

The moment that happens and they respond to the remark, I just became a *person*! My chances of getting an appointment with them have gone up by a factor of ten. They may respond to my remark with a statement like 'Just reasonable?' I respond back with "Yes, not cheap, not expensive, just reasonable." Or "Yes it's better than the alternative." and they will usually laugh.

Now keep in mind, although the explanation seems long, all of this takes place in less than eight seconds. If you don't believe this works, try it for a couple of days yourself. Every time someone you encounter asks you 'How are you?' respond with "Reasonable" and watch their reaction. As you use the approach more you will be surprised by the wide and varied responses you will get from people and if you pay attention their response will give you some insight as to how they are feeling at the moment in time. For example, if they respond with 'Just Reasonable?' they are usually in a good mood. On the other hand if they say, 'Yeah, I know what you mean.' Then their day is not going so well.

I have found that by setting yourself away from the pack and above the fray, it will make you a more colorful person. It also gets you much further in life, than being, like most, one of the many shades of gray.

"Do not follow where the path may lead. Go, instead, where there is no path and leave a trail."
                                                    ~**Ralph Waldo Emerson**

Chapter 9

Pound Puppy Flies

A friend of mine, Jeff Olson, wrote an extraordinary book, *The Slight Edge*. If you are planning a diet or working on personal development, I recommend you read his book before starting any of these endeavors. Without stealing the thunder away from his book, Mr. Olson discusses something called *The Slight Edge*. Simply put, *The Slight Edge* refers to how the effects of the simple, little, seemingly unimportant decisions, made over a long period, will have a compounding effect of either great success or great failure. So how does a dog go from being a puppy in the dog pound to becoming a Frisbee catching wonder? This is the story, and this story shows the power and simplicity of *The Slight Edge*.

I have always had a love for animals. As a child, I always wanted a pet; but to my dismay when I asked my mother if I could have one she would always say, 'When you have your own home you can have all the pets you want.' Needless to say, I had very few pets as a child.

You can imagine my excitement when the day finally arrived; I had a home of my own. I then realized I could now have my very own pet, and I decided to get a dog.

Knowing the pound had plenty of dogs who needed homes, I decided this was where I was going to get my dog.

When I arrived at the pound, I asked where the puppy section was. They ushered me over to the area where all the puppies were – and there were lots and lots of puppies. Though there were many puppies, they completely ignored me, except one. The puppy looked right at me and seemingly said, "I'm coming home with you." And that he did! I brought the little dog home with me and named him Toby.

Toby was half Dachshund, half Manchester Terrier, and all energy, even though he was quite small. In fact, he was too small to be left alone in the backyard. So, when I went to work the next day I left him in the laundry room. I put out some newspapers, food and water there for him, and off to work I went. When I came home from work, I sat down on the couch, and heard the little dog whimpering in the laundry room. My guilt got the best of me and I said to myself, "Well, you wanted a dog; you got a dog, now you'd better go exercise it." I had made a commitment and now I had to live up to it. There is a saying, *"Commitment is doing the thing you said you'd do, long after the feeling in which you said it in has passed."* This was one of those moments. I had committed to having a dog, so I committed to making sure he was properly taken care of.

I took him out to the backyard, and at first, I tried to get him to run around with me. After a while, this began to feel like exercise to me and since exercise was not something I was fond of, I tried to come up with a better idea. I wondered if I could teach Toby to fetch. Over the next couple of days, I taught him to fetch a ball. While it was fun for a while, soon I became bored. I wondered, what else I could teach him to fetch. I looked around my house and found an old Frisbee in my closet.

While Toby was willing, the Frisbee was about as big as he was. It was so big, when he would try to carry it he would trip over it. To avoid tripping he would flip it upside-down. Then the problem was, when it was flipped upside-down and he tried to carry it the Frisbee blocked his view. In order to be able to see with the Frisbee in his mouth, he would lope like a baby deer. It was extremely endearing to watch.

Being as lazy as I am, the next thing I found as a new dog owner was an upside-down Frisbee makes an excellent dog bowl. Once I discovered this handy fact, I would fill the Frisbee with dog food and leave it with Toby in the laundry room while I went off to work. As time went on Toby grew very fond of the Frisbee. Every day when I came home from work, he would be waiting for me, Frisbee in mouth, to take him to play.

We started out playing Frisbee in the backyard. As he got bigger and bigger and I got better and better at throwing the Frisbee, we moved our game of Frisbee to the front yard. Then we moved the game to the next-door-neighbor's yard, then the neighbor's, neighbor's yard, then the neighbor's, neighbor's, neighbor's yard. Then… we ran out of yards. When we finally ran out of yards, I decided we should move our game to the park. From then on every day when I came home from work, without fail, Toby and I would get in the car and go to the park. As the months went on Toby continued to grow and get stronger and faster, and I continued to get better and better at throwing the Frisbee (This was a function of *The Slight Edge* at work).

One day when I threw the Frisbee, the wind caught it and held it in the air. Toby got to the Frisbee before it began to fall and started barking at it. Then, he did something amazing. He jumped for it! It turns out half of all dogs will not jump for a Frisbee because they know it is going to land anyways, the other half, know it will land also but jump out of pure enthusiasm. Well, he was very enthusiastic and I thought it was very cute. I wondered if I could get him to do it again. Sure enough, I could. As time went on I threw the Frisbee higher and higher and he jumped higher still.

One day while we were playing Frisbee in the park, a little boy came by on his bicycle and watched us. He thought it was neat and asked if we were there every day. I said, "Yes we were." He said, 'Can I bring a couple of my friends?' I said "Of course." The next day he came with a couple friends, so now we had a small audience. Toby completely ignored them. As time went on an audience of a few turned to ten, turned to dozens, turned into a hundred, and finally turned into almost two hundred people coming to watch us every day. Over time, Toby had become accustomed to an audience and the amount of people and noise did not bother him at all.

After one of our play sessions in the park, a woman came up to me and asked, 'Did you know there is a contest for this?' I said, "You're kidding!" She said, 'No. They're holding it this Saturday in Long Beach.' Well, needless to say, we were there.

The morning of the competition, we went down to Long Beach and signed in with about 300 other dogs. As we watched all the dogs practice, I noticed most of them only jumped up a foot or two, but because they stretched out so long, like sheepdogs, they appeared to be much higher in the air than they really were. Because of this observation, when it was our turn for warm-ups, I said "No." Knowing how high Toby could jump compared to the other dogs I wanted to keep the element of surprise in our favor. We were the last ones to compete that day.

Each time the other dogs performed, everyone would clap for each other. When our turn came, for the first couple of throws, I threw just like everyone else. Toby stretched out only a foot or so to catch the Frisbee and everyone clapped for us too. For our third and final throw, I decided enough was enough; it was time to show everyone what Toby could really do.

I took the Frisbee and pretended to throw it hard to my right. Toby thought I threw it and took off in the direction (toward what would be first base if we were on a baseball field and if I were standing on home plate). I then threw the Frisbee to my left (where third base would have been). Toby was headed toward first, the Frisbee was headed toward third, and the audience sighed in disappointment. Once Toby saw the Frisbee, without pause or worry, he took a sharp left and headed toward second base. As the Frisbee flew over third base, it took a sharp right toward second base. Toby took a flying leap, caught the Frisbee about six or seven feet in the air, did a full somersault and landed flat on his feet with the Frisbee in his mouth. No one applauded. Instead, we were greeted with stunned awe. The audience knew the competition had just ended. No one could compete with Toby. Toby won that competition and every competition thereafter.

Someone once said, *"Titles don't spend well at the Super Market."* While Toby was an astonishing Frisbee catcher, his talent did not equate to dollars until he was actually discovered in a most unusual fashion.

In 1978, Toby and I moved to Hawaii. At the time, part of the requirements for bringing a pet with you to the islands was the animal needed to be quarantined for three months. During quarantine, the dogs were housed in a facility where the kennels were roughly eight feet tall. I went to visit Toby almost every day while he was in quarantine.

One day when I was visiting him, a man approached me and asked if Toby was my dog. He said, 'What's the deal with your dog? Every time I walk past, he jumps up in the air, all the way to the top of the kennel, and just keeps jumping over and over again. I've never seen a dog jump so high in my life.' I told him, "Well, Toby is actually one of the Competitive Champion Frisbee Catching Dogs." He said, 'Really?' And I said, "Yes."

Apparently, the story spread to a Hawaiian baseball team promoter who was responsible for finding performers to entertain the crowd during the 7th inning stretches at their home games. I met with him as soon as Toby was released from quarantine. We performed a demonstration for him at a local park. Unquestionably, the promoter was more than impressed by Toby, and the team was thrilled to have him perform at their stadium.

While it was nice, at the time it was actually against the law for animals to enter the Aloha Stadium. Nonetheless, they still wanted Toby to perform. In order for it to be possible, Toby first had to meet everyone, all the way from the City Council Members and the Mayor to the Governor of Hawaii. After getting through all the red tape, Toby was finally permitted to perform at the Aloha Stadium. With all the *Red Tape* that had occurred, we had created quite the media frenzy. That much hype drew a tremendous crowd to Toby's first game appearance. People were so curious; they had to see for themselves what all the fuss was about.

Furthermore, the baseball team did not have a lot of extra money in their budget, especially for 7th inning stretch performers. I suggested Toby could get a sponsor, providing the stadium would allow the sponsor to be promoted on the billboard during the game. The stadium agreed and Toby went on to be paid anywhere from $1,000 to $2,000 for a four and a half minute performance making him one of the highest paid dogs in the world.

After his first stadium performance, we had requests lined up around the block including, Bank of Hawaii, M & M Trucking and the Pepsi Cola / Seven Up Bottling Company of Honolulu (which went on to become one of our biggest sponsors). Toby was featured in many newspapers and periodicals. He was paid for personal appearances, that went on to include autograph signings at which he would literally put his paw print on books and items for his fans.

I would like to mention another important factor at this time. There came a point where I realized how great Toby could be and I saw this point long before everyone else did. In fact, I started talking to people and telling them about what he could do as if he was already doing it. I was so emphatic about it my close friend would say to me, 'You shouldn't say that. He can't really do the things you are telling people.' I was visualizing what could be, not just what was. Toby ended up exceeding my vision.

Remember: *What the heart believes…*
The mind achieves!

Toby's success and talent is truly a *Slight Edge* story and an example of how simple little things compounded over time can compile to be a great success.

Chapter 9

Hi Tech Magic!

This is the story of Mastervoice
"Everywhere, but Nowhere"

How is it a guy who flunked computer programming in college and was a magician professionally, ended up inventing a technology, that had such a huge effect on how the world operates? On one hand, I am the last person in the world one would think would have done this. Yet on the other hand, I am exactly the person who should have done what I am about to share with you.

Instead of buying me a toy train set when I was a young child, my parents bought me a chemistry set and a Lionel

Electronics Kit. This Lionel Electronics Kit was designed to teach a child about electronics, relays, circuits, and things of that nature. As a matter of fact, to this day I still have pieces from the kit in my garage. As a young kid, I was able to do some pretty amazing things with my little electronic kit.

When I was in junior high school, I was able to set up a switch system that allowed me to shine a flashlight from my bedroom door, this would start a relay, that would then turn on my bedroom lamp and the lamp would stay on until I waved my hand to turn it off.

Here is how it worked: I hung a flashlight just inside my bedroom door. When I walked into my room, I would shine the flashlight across the room onto a little mirror. The mirror would reflect the light onto a Dixie Cup, which had a photo electric cell that was connected to a 9-volt battery. The 9-volt battery was then connected to a relay, that was connected to one side of the wiring of my lamp and would turn the lamp on. The light from the lamp would power the solar cell in the Dixie Cup and would keep the lamp lit until I would wave my hand over the solar cell when I was ready for bed, this would cause the lamp to turn off.

Additionally, while still in junior high school, I created another modern convenience for my bedroom. One morning after I had left for school, it began to rain. Unfortunately, I had forgotten to close my bedroom window. Consequently, the rain came into my bedroom.

My parents were less than pleased about it, and I was in trouble. To insure this did not happen again, I built little rain sensors attached to motors so when it rained, if my windows had been left open, they would close. Thus, my bedroom stayed dry, and I stayed out of trouble, whether or not I remembered to close my window before leaving the house.

During my days as a magician, one evening, I threw a party at my home. As it began to get dark that evening, I started to walk around my home to turn on some lights. As I was doing this, one of my friends who had a few to drinks, began to tease me. He said, 'What kind of magician are you? You have to get up to turn the lights on in your house?' Soon the rest of my friends began to tease me about the same thing. As irritating as it was, it did not take long before I realized they were right. A magician should not have to get up to turn on the lights! Now, not many people would have done anything about this. Many would have simply laughed it off as nothing more than a few friends giving another friend a hard time about something, just as friends do. However, I made a different choice. I said to myself, "You know what? They are right! I am a magician. I should not have to get up to turn the lights on. I'll show them!"

I started thinking about how I would go about being able to turn the lights on in my home without getting up and walking around the house to turn them on one by one, room by room. Keep in mind this was back in the middle of the 1970s. Computers did not really exist yet. They most certainly were not in the realm of the average person by any stretch of the imagination. Moreover, they were about the size of buildings.

In all this brainstorming, I remembered in the black and white TV show, *The Adams Family*, there was a character called *Thing*. He was 'everywhere, but nowhere.' This really stuck out in my mind, so I kept referring back to this little slogan, 'everywhere, but nowhere' as I went about trying to come up with a way to *magically* turn the lights on in my home.

Then, in 1979, I saw a movie, starring Julie Christy, called *Demon Seed*. In the movie there was a computer called Protious 4. Protious 4 was a computer connected to the house. The main character could actually talk to the house and tell it what to do. When I saw it, I just about jumped out of my skin. I thought to myself, "Wow! That's it! A Computerized Thing!" With this idea, I was off and running. Now I really knew what had to be created.

Unfortunately, at the time, computers were not even in the price range of the average person, so they could afford to own one, which made the idea of mine ahead of the available technology. So I didn't really do much and for about a year and a half I just sat and waited, hoping technology would advance far enough to make this idea of mine a bit more possible.

Then in 1980, a computer company called Commodore came out with a computer called the Commodore P.E.T. It had a whopping 32k of memory and two, 550-kilobyte drives, which together gave you one megabyte of virtual memory. It cost about $8,000 to purchase.

Being the highest paid magician in the world at the time, I was earning about $1,000 per day. This was only about eight days worth of pay. Knowing nothing about computers, other than I was going to need one if I was going to make all of this any kind of reality, I bought one.

I brought it home to my office upstairs and for the next three months, I ate whatever would fit under the door, essentially a pizza diet, and did not really leave the room. I diligently educated myself on how computers worked and what they did as I began to create this invention of mine. For the most part, I had it working. There were still a few things I did not know how to do.

One day one of the local computer stores called me up. They had a new programmer working there from Germany. His name was Franz. They said he did not speak a lot of English; he was lonely and wanted someone to talk to, so they thought of me. They invited me to come have lunch with him, and I accepted their invitation.

At lunch, I performed a little magic for him and we seemed to get along pretty well. One day Franz called me up and asked if he could come over. I said, "Sure."

He came over. As I watched him on the computer I realized, "Wow! This guy is totally brilliant!"

So I pulled out everything I had been working on and explained to him what I was trying to do, what I had managed to accomplish thus far, and where I had become stuck. He said to me, 'It won't work.' I argued, "Yes! It will work." He then replied, 'I am a genius, and I am telling you, this will not work.'

Now, he actually was a genius, so he could say that. However, sometimes it does not matter how smart someone is. They still cannot see what another person sees. So I said again, "It will work. And if you make it work, I will have you on national television tomorrow night." His response to my proposal and me was, 'Bubble Talk!' When translated, essentially meant "b.s." He continued on to say, 'You Americans, you all talk big, but you don't really do anything.' To that I replied, "Franz, what do you have to lose? It is a Saturday afternoon, and we don't have anything else to do. Why don't you try it? It should only take you about 2 hours."

He said he would give it a shot, and he proceeded to try what I had suggested. Lo and behold, to his surprise, it worked! Two hours later, if you had driven past my house you would have thought there had been a triple homicide, judging by the number of media vans that were in front of my house and lined up all the way around the block. We had CBS, ABC, NBC, national television, and Channel 5, **11** and Channel 13 local stations. All the major news stations were covering our story.

We had created the first human interactive machine in the world. It could see, hear, think, speak, had a personality definable by its owner, was quad lingual (it understood up to four languages simultaneously), and could speak any language on earth in 15 seconds. Best of all it just plugged into the wall of a normal house. It operated in four modes of operation: time, touch, situation, and voice. It knew days of the week, months of the year, seasons, holidays and even if-then conditions. For example: turn the lights off at 10:00 p.m. but not if we are having a party. It knew if it was raining not to water the lawn. In the fourth mode, you could talk to it by voice.

However, at the time I had to invent voice recognition technology because it did not yet exist. Another characteristic, which made our invention extremely unique, was when it spoke back to you, it spoke in an exactly human perfect voice, and not the robotic non-human voice people were familiar with. It sounded just like a human being, complete with a personality.

God's on the Phone

The publicity we received from our invention was just absolutely incredible! News channels were introducing our story as a scientific breakthrough. Franz was extremely excited that I had actually kept my word and landed him on to national television.

We had been noticed and recognized by everyone. Just when we thought it couldn't get any better it did. The very next day the phone rang. The man on the other end was the CEO of the biggest computer company in the world at the time. Today it would have been as if Mr. Bill Gates, himself, was on the other line. I looked at Franz and said, "God is on the phone."

We were so excited he had actually called us. He told us how he had seen us on the news and our story was very impressive. Then he went on to say how his company was very excited for an opportunity to work with us. He would like us to go ahead and box up everything we had done and ship it over to them so they could take a look at it and see how we could put it together as a product. In that moment, God, grew horns and a tail.

Did he really think we were stupid enough to just hand over everything we had worked so hard to create? I was very polite about it and simply agreed and said we would get around to shipping it when we could. Of course, I had no real intention of shipping everything off to them so they could just rip us off.

A couple of days later he called back again. I just played it off saying I had just been so busy since all of the TV exposure I had not had a chance to send it off yet. Then he went on to tell me how they really wanted a chance to evaluate the product. He said someone from their company would be by in the morning to check it out. He asked me if it was ok. I said "Sure," and I did not really think much more about it. The next morning at 9 a.m., my doorbell rang.

The gentleman at my door was a representative from the computer company. He handed me his business card. This person actually had a PHD in Computer Software. The Company had flown him out to evaluate our technology.

I politely escorted him upstairs to my office where our invention was. I sat him down and gave him two simple rules before he could begin his evaluation. Rule number one was he could not open the box. We had already physically taped the cardboard box shut so the electronic components inside could not be seen. Rule number two was he could not 'list the program.' He agreed. Then I went over to the other side of the room to work on other things while he did his evaluation.

It was not more than thirty or forty seconds after I had left him to his evaluation before he called me over to help him. He said, 'Excuse me, your computer is frozen.' To which I replied, "Perhaps you did not understand the rules. I told you, you could not open the box because we had taped it closed. I told you, you *could not* list the programs. I did not say to you, not to list the programs. We had removed the *List Command* from the bios in the computer (the computer's operating system). Therefore, the list command no longer existed so listing the programs was not an option. When you tried to list the programs, you caused the computer to freeze."

After this occurrence, he had a lot more respect for us. At this point, in time there were very few people who knew how to get into a computer and make those kinds of changes. In fact, if I had been smarter, I would have created DOS and been "Bill Gates," because I had the same ideas and concepts at this point in time. However, I was going in a different direction.

He then went on to explore and evaluate the computer, as he was supposed to, for about thirty minutes. When he was done, he walked over to me, handed me his card again, and said, 'You are going to get a glowing report from me to the company.' Then he looked at me very seriously and said, 'Between you and me, be very careful with this. A lot of people are going to try to steal it.' Then he left.

Of course, a few days later we received another call from the president of that large computer company offering us a few things. However, it still was a little too suspicious for us. Originally, all my friends were saying, 'Hey. You are just a dumb magician who got lucky. You should take the money and run.' And that was exactly what I was going to do. But after all the interest and back and forth with this company, I had calculated how much money we would need and decided we should just go ahead and do it ourselves. This is when I decided to take our company to the next level and began my quest for the $2.2 Million Dollars, that this project would require.

* * *

The company was called Mastervoice and the product (as named by the press) was Butler-In-A-Box.

In order to create a successful company, I had calculated we would need an initial investment of 2.2 million dollars. Keep in mind; my credentials consisted of being a professional magician who had flunked computer programming in college. All my friends thought I was out of my mind.

For the next two and a half years, I proceeded to be kicked out of the best boardrooms in America, and all over the world. They all said to me, in one fashion or another, the same thing, 'Gus that's pretty silly. No one is going to talk to machines.' None of these rejections stopped me from continuing to ask. Imagine how many people give up on things after only a few days, weeks, or months of trying.

Eventually I stumbled into a very wealthy individual who had apparently been following my progress and efforts, unbeknownst to me. He invited me to meet with his board. At the meeting, his people informed me they had reviewed my plans and proposals and they had decided to fund me. They were willing to invest 1.5 million dollars.

I too had my little entourage there with me at the meeting, and they were very excited about this, especially after all of the *No's* I had received over the last two and a half years. Unfortunately, it was not the correct amount of money we needed. We needed 2.2 million dollars. 1.5 million dollars was not going to be enough; it would only be enough to get us into trouble, knowing this, I looked up and said, "No. I need 2.2 million." At the moment, I thought everyone in the boardroom was going to drop dead. They were all absolutely stunned. Yet, I stayed firm. I knew what I needed, and 1.5 million dollars was not it.

Two days later, they called me to say, 'You have your 2.2 million dollars.'

The rest is history. The technology, product, and company were created. To this day, the Butler -In-A-Box, serial #1 resides in the Smithsonian Museum in Washington D.C.

Throughout the entire process, I talked to everyone I knew about my invention and all it would do. I spoke about it as if it was already in existence. All of my friends and family would always ask the same thing, "Why do you talk like that? It can't do that. Why are you exaggerating?" However, in my mind, I was not exaggerating at all; remember I did the same thing with Toby. I believed it would do it. In the end, it did all I had said it would and even more than I had imagined.

The value of being able to believe in yourself when no one else does is powerful beyond measure. Additionally, one of the greatest factors, which separate those who succeed from those who do not, is those who succeed are willing to hang on long enough to see the payout of their efforts.

Many people say they believe I am incredibly smart and brilliant. Truth be told, I do not think I am as smart as they say I am. I believe it just boils down to the fact I am more stubborn than most people are, and I do not quit when most people would. I do believe if people would stick, with whatever it is they are trying to accomplish, a little longer, they would be able to achieve a lot more success.

Furthermore, this invention actually saved the lives of several individuals. What if I had never been born? What if I had not taken action and had given up when everyone told me to? Therein is the power, once again, of positive choice.

Action: "Do not be too timid and squeamish about your actions. All life is an experiment. The more experiments you make the better. What if they are a little course and you may get your coat soiled or torn? What if you do fail, and get fairly rolled in the dirt once or twice? Up again, you shall never be so afraid of a tumble."

- Ralph Waldo Emerson

Fish Food

Once you invent something and you validate your feelings, that you are capable of doing it, a completely new world of possibilities opens up to you.

After the completion of my first major invention, Butler-In-A-Box, I did many other minor inventions, most of which were accessories to other inventions or specific product line expansions. I received a lot of press and publicity for my inventions. As a result of all that exposure, my reputation grew to precede me throughout the industry.

During those years, my company and I would take our product line to the Consumer Electronics Trade Show. This show is one of the largest electronics shows around the world with hundreds and hundreds of companies. Everyone who makes electronics, whether it is Samsung, Texas Instruments, Sony, Panasonic, you-name-it, they are there.

Each year it happens to be in Las Vegas, Nevada. Apparently, at the show, there were a couple of people walking around the show asking if anyone knew of anybody who did unusual and out-of-the-ordinary electronic design, creation, and installation. Evidently, in all of the names they gathered, my name came up more than once. As a matter of fact, my name was the only name, which came up more than once.

Soon after the show, they contacted me. A meeting was scheduled at my home to meet with me. After they saw my home automation system in action, with voice-activated recognition, they realized if I could do all of that, then surely I could assist them.

Initially they hired me to do all of the audio and video systems, including wiring, for the inside of a submarine. The reason this was such a unique task was essentially they wanted a home theater system inside a submarine. Now a home theater works great inside a square building or room, but when you try to put it in a long metal tube, it becomes challenging to maintain the audio quality of a surround sound home theater system. The audio challenges, which those circumstances created, were something most people and companies were not equipped to manage. However, this was not a problem for me.

One day while we were sitting in one of our meetings, they mentioned they came from the glass bottom boat industry. In that industry, they made a lot of money by selling fish food to people so they could feed the fish. They asked me if I had any ideas on how they could accomplish it in the submarine. I said, "Well yeah. Just open the window and hand them the food." Of course, they all looked at me as if I had a few loose screws of my own until they realized I was kidding.

Then I said, "O.K. What's the problem?" They wanted to figure out how to feed the fish from inside the submarine. I asked them what they had already tried.

They had tried all kinds of things, but nothing had worked. So I said, "Well, I don't know, but I think I can make it work. If nothing else, I can do a feasibility study. I will charge you about $2,000 and at the end of one week; I will tell you whether or not it can be done. If it can be done, I will give you a fundamental demonstration of how it would work." They said O.K. and they wrote me a check for $2,000.

From there I went to work on trying to figure out the plausibility of making it work. At the end of the week, I had plausibility and a demonstration and I invited them over to show it to them. After the demo they said, 'Great! How much will this cost?' I gave them a six-figure quote. They said, 'OK,' and wrote me a check for about half.

After the meeting, I took all of my work and this idea and I presented it to my company, my controller, engineers, programmers, etc. To my surprise, my colleagues were actually upset with me. I said, "Why are you guys upset with me? This is great! We landed the deal." Then they asked, 'How are you going to do it?' To which I replied, "I don't know yet." They were even further upset by my answer. 'How can you take all that money when you don't know?'

Here's the point. Yes. At the time, I had no idea how I was actually going to make it work. This is not what was important. What was important was I knew it was possible, remember I had already done a successful feasibility test. This is the key. You do not have to know how to get from California to New York; you just need to know you can. Once you know it is feasible, you start looking for the hows, by bus, by plane, by car, by roller-skates. The exact details do not really matter as long as you decide to get started and do it. The hows will reveal themselves along the way.

The first thing I did was to gather my technical department. I sat them down and said, "All right. This is what we have to do." To my surprise, they were at a total loss. They had no idea how to make this work. They spent almost two days just staring at things having no idea how we could pull this off. Finally, with no progress I said, "Alright. You guys just go home." It was my company's policy to be closed from Christmas through New Years and this happened right around Christmas.

During the holiday break, I decided I was going to do it myself. Even though I did not have the engineering or programming degrees they had, I did have quite a bit of knowledge. I also had those years with my little Lionel Electronics Kit back during my younger years, and I had become very good at tinkering with things and making them work.

I approached this task with one of my strongest philosophies. *Start with the known, and then work to the unknown.* I share this philosophy with people, all the time. Start with what you do know, and then slowly work, step by step, toward what you do not know.

Suddenly you can create something from nothing through your experience of moving through this process. This is exactly what I did.

From my plausibility study, I knew piece "x" could do what I needed and I worked backwards from there. By the time the holiday break was over and everyone came back to work in early January, I had a table covered end-to-end with all of the electronic components. I had every single piece in place functioning and working as it was supposed to. Then I brought the engineers in. I said, "Here you go guys. It is done. It works. Now make a schematic and make it look professional. I'll talk to you later."

We then installed this system into the submarine called The Nautilus in Catalina Island, California. This little invention of ours became the first automated fish food firing system in the world. This feature allows children at each window in the submarine to push a button and shoot food out to the fish. My system also included an inventory control system for the management so they could keep track of everything, that was happening.

When you think about shooting food out of a submarine and at fish, it does not sound as challenging as it actually was. First of all, each element must be approved by the Coast Guard. You cannot just put anything you want on a boat. It also must essentially be bulletproof. It must be unwaveringly dependable. It is not very easy to run a part out to a submarine on an island in the middle of nowhere every time something breaks or malfunctions.

This system turned out to be a huge success. I have been told I am going to get the opportunity to build a few more of them and install them in a few other locations around the world so thousands of other people will get to enjoy them as well.

What I hope you have learned from this chapter is you should not worry about what everyone else tells you. Especially, when it comes to what you can or cannot do. There will always be people ready to criticize you. Furthermore, when you are in doubt about a problem, whether it is figuring out how to cook something, fix something, or anything else; remember my saying *"Start with a known and work to the unknown."* If you do it, you will be able to walk yourself through almost any problem, which you encounter.

Remember: The difference between dreams and reality is effort! - Gus Searcy

Chapter 11

The Ring!

Louis Pasteur said, ***"Chance favors the prepared mind,"*** but one must have a positive attitude and outlook about chance for it to be effective. I always try to keep an open mind about everything. Most people are quick to say "no" to most things. My philosophy is: ***Never say "no" until you "know" what you are saying "no" to.*** A few years ago, this philosophy was put to the test. Here is what happened…

One day I was sitting at my desk when I received a phone call, which had been transferred to me in error. On the phone was a young woman, (we will call her Liz) who asked me if I had watched the DVD she gave me. Of course, I had not received a DVD and she had the wrong person, but I was polite and understanding of her plight.

Once she realized she had the wrong person, instead of hanging up, as most people would have done she said, 'You have been very nice about this. May I get you a DVD and explain what this is all about?'

She had such a good attitude about her I said yes. Over the next six months, she followed up with me every few days. Finally I said to myself, "If this girl spends half as much time helping me succeed in her business, as she has spent trying to get me to join her business, it might be worth a shot and give it a try." Ninety days later, I attained the top level of Executive Director with the company and 32 months later became a "Ring Earner" for the company. A "Ring Earner" is someone who makes a documented $100,000.00 income in a 12 month time period from home, which in my case was mostly passive. Imagine if I had just said "No!" Look what I would have said "no" to!

The Company was a network marketing company and a great one to boot. I know some of you are saying about now… "Oh, it's one of those pyramid schemes." I tell you now, *that* thought is brainwashing from corporate America and is a pure case of the pot calling the kettle black. It is in fact the other way around. Take any large corporation and take a good look at their structure. At the top, they have the president, then a couple of vice presidents, then regional managers and so on down to the everyday workers. Can anyone see a pyramid here? What are the percentages of worker at the bottom reaching the top of that company's pyramid? Slim and none, I am sure you would agree.

In network marketing, you are paid for your own personal efforts as well as those of the team you built. Just like insurance or real estate brokers, it is definitely not an illegal pyramid. In today's economy the average family needs an additional income stream but has little time or energy to get a third or fourth job. Network marketing is the answer and the best-kept secret in America today.

In network marketing, you build a team and help them grow and prosper. The better they do, the better you do. There is a saying in this industry that I have found to be very true, it states: *"If you help people get what they want then you will get everything that you want."* The problem I discovered is many people are reluctant to help people who are not in their organization, as they receive no financial gain for doing so. This is unfortunate and short sighted on their part. They do not realize by helping the marketplace they help themselves as well. I am personally not money motivated (never have been) and helping people whether I am compensated or not has never been part of my thought process. Call it Karma or "what goes around comes around," but whenever I do a good thing, usually in a short period of time, an equal or better good is returned to me. The following is a story and perfect example of this. It is called: *'The Slight Edge Meets The Secret…'*

The Slight Edge

In order to truly grasp the magnitude of this story you must first understand two unique principles. The first, as I had mentioned in the chapter about Toby, is the principle of *The Slight Edge*. Mr. Jeff Olson wrote a book called *The Slight Edge*. This book explains the principle very well, and I recommend this book to anyone who is seeking something, be it financial success or to lose five pounds. Throughout this book, I have referred to this principle. Now allow me to give you a few clear examples before I tell this next story.

Let's say I have an identical twin and he and I go to lunch. He orders a salad and an ice tea with no sugar. I have a hamburger, an order of fries, a vanilla shake, and an apple turnover. After the meal, will there be any difference between the two of us? No. What if we ate those same meals for a week? Would there be a real difference? Probably not. What about if we each ate the meal for six whole years? You would absolutely see a difference. This would be the effect of *The Slight Edge*. A seemly insignificant decision compounded over time makes all the difference in the world.

As another example, let's take two associates in our business, one man, and one woman. They go out today and each shares our business with two people. At the end of the day, would there be any difference in their business? No. The next day she shares the information with two people again and the other associate (he) shares it with no one. Any difference in their business? Not really. The next day they each share the information with two people. The next day she tells two, he tells none. The next day she tells two, he tells none. At the end of the week, is there any difference in their business? No, no real difference. If it continues two or three years from now, is it going to make a difference? Yes, a huge difference!

I am so far ahead of many others in our company simply because I have gotten more 'No's' than most people. Those 'No's lead me to more 'Yes's' which is what earned me the $100,000 ring.

The Secret

The second principle that is present in this next story is what is now commonly referred to as: *The Law of Attraction. This phrase was popularized because of a book and film called: The Secret.* A lot of the same ideas and philosophies can also be found in the Bible. Again, the book, The Secret covers this principle well, and I recommend it. In the book and the movie, it does not look like any of this came from the Bible and other books, but it did.

The principle of *The Law of Attraction* says everything we know, our bodies, this book, the chair you are sitting on, and our thoughts are all made of the same stuff in the universe. Furthermore, our thoughts are powerful and they are the source of creation. When you send a thought out to the universe, if it is strong enough, even if it is not conscious, it will manifest. I learned *The Law of Attraction* when I was seven years old, as I shared with you in Chapter 2.

It has been stated that: ***"What you <u>think</u> about, and <u>thank</u> about, will come about."*** and you need to understand that the little seemingly insignificant things compound over time and make all the difference.

The Slight Edge Meets *The Secret*

For the last several years I have trained at weekly meetings, and I always tell everyone to put magnetic signs on their cars. When I tell people this, I most commonly get one of two responses. Response A is: 'I am not putting those stupid magnetic signs on my nice car.' Or Response B: 'You can't put those signs on your car if you have a dumpy car.' To them, I submit this: I have a 1998 Jeep Grand Cherokee that is washed when God washes it. Being as I live in Southern California, it is not washed very often. However, I do have those little magnetic signs on the sides of my Jeep.

One evening, I was doing a business presentation and at the end of the presentation, a young man came up to me and said, 'Would you help me?' I said, "Sure. I'd be glad to help you." Nervously, he replied, 'But I'm not on your team.' This meant I would not make any money by helping him. To which I said, "Well, that's alright. It doesn't matter. I'll help you anyway." We set up an appointment to meet the next Wednesday.

At our meeting, I found out he had been stuck at a particular position in our company for about two and a half years, and could not get to the next level. He really wanted to get to the next level, and saw how fast I had been promoted through our company ranks. He was thinking that maybe I could help him. I let him know I would be glad to help him, but he needed to know I worked a little differently than most. If I was going to help, he was simply going to have to follow my lead. I did not want to have to argue with him over everything. It needed to be an efficient process, kind of like, "Wax on, Wax off." (Movie *The Karate Kid* reference, if you did not catch it.) He said, 'Whatever you say, I'll do it.' After working with me two and a half weeks he had attained the promotion to the top company level he wanted, he has held this level in the company ever since. He was even awarded a certificate at our national convention as the number one seller in our entire company for a specific product we offer.

Because of his promotion, his sponsor received a promotion as well. Coincidently, at the time they were participating in a contest in our company, where if you reached the next level you won an all-expense-paid cruise. His sponsor won the cruise. I did the work, and she won the cruise. No big deal, this was fine with me. It is not the money that motivates me.

One day his sponsor called me up and said, 'Hey, I saw how you impacted my associate. I was wondering if you would come speak to my team at an event we are having. I would love to have them hear from you. I appreciate all the work you did to help the young man. Maybe hearing from you could help them too,' so I thought to myself for a minute. Well, let's see. They are not on my team; it is a Saturday afternoon, I have other things I could be doing; and I don't make any money if I help them succeed... "O.K."

After I did my little presentation to her group Saturday afternoon a lady walked up to me and said, 'Would you be my workout partner?' I said, "Well, O.K." Then she said, 'Well, I'm not on your team. In fact, I am not even with your company.' Apparently I looked confused, so she explained, 'You seem to know what you are doing, and I could use a little direction. I was wondering if you would be my business workout partner and mentor me.' So I thought to myself a minute. Well let's see. She is not a part of my business, I will not make any money out of this; I have other things to do, and she is not even in my company... "O.K." We set up an appointment to meet the next Wednesday.

Keep in mind; I am not making any money on any of this. At this point, is any of this helping me in any way? No. Not in a way, any of us can see. However, *The Slight Edge* is working in the background. And I <u>do</u> have those 'stupid' car signs on my Jeep!

Wednesday came, and I met with her. At our meeting, I discovered she had the exclusive rights to a high-end cosmetic line. This very high-end product line was imported from Korea. It is very expensive and worked very well. She was trying to break into the American market. After spending about two and a half hours with her, I had a good sense of what she was trying to accomplish. I then advised her if she wanted to break into the American market, she was going to have to go where money didn't matter. This meant she would need to get her line into a medical skin care clinic where they do Botox and procedures of a similar nature. After the advice she asked, 'Well how do I do it?' I said, "I don't know, but I will figure it out." So she said, 'O.K. Let me at least buy you lunch for all your effort.' I agreed, but I had somewhere else I needed to be not too much later, so we decided to drive separate cars.

She stepped into her shiny silver Mercedes SUV, I got into my dumpy Jeep with my stupid little magnetic signs, and I proceeded to follow her. She pulled out of the parking lot and made a left turn. I pulled up to the road, looked both ways before pulling forward. Before I pulled forward, my phone rang so I looked down. It was "Liz," calling (the girl who had recruited me into the business), so I had to take her call.

Note: (From this moment forward everything is documented because, remember, I was on the phone with Liz, and she heard everything.)

So we were on the phone chatting, and it went something like this: Me: "Hey Liz, hold on a sec I am following a lady (and I start following the silver Mercedes SUV down the street). Yeah, it is kind of a non-work workday. I am helping someone with something outside of the company. Yes, I will be at the training event this week. Yes, I am up to date on my work. Yes I will qualify for my rank this month, don't worry," She was such a mother hen! All the while, I was following the shiny silver Mercedes SUV.

The silver SUV turned into a shopping center, so I turned into the same one. It parked, so I parked right next to it. I looked over. It was not her. Apparently, when I looked down to answer my phone, a different silver Mercedes SUV pulled in front of me, and I proceeded to follow the wrong silver SUV. (I was still on the phone with Liz.)
I said to Liz, "Oh my gosh, Liz, I followed the wrong car. What am I going to do?" Liz asked if I knew the woman's phone number. I did not. I said, "Hang on a minute. Let me pull over to an area where there are no other cars so in case she circles back to find me maybe she would spot my (stupid) little magnetic signs."

So I am sitting in my car in a parking lot not near any other cars, talking to Liz on the phone and suddenly I hear a *knock, knock, knock* on my window. I looked over and there was a man standing there. He looked at me, pointed at my magnet sign, then pointed at me and shrugged his shoulders. So I rolled down my window, about 1 inch. Then he said, 'Do you represent this company?' And I said, "Yes." Then he said, 'Do you know what you are doing?' And I said, "I better." Then he said, 'Well, good, I want it!'

Meanwhile Liz was still on the phone with me. She heard him and said, 'Well, sounds like you have to go to work. I'll let you go.' So I got off the phone, got out of the car, and started to talk to this man. I gave him a brochure and set an appointment to meet with him the following Wednesday. As we were about to go our separate ways, I asked him, "By the way. What do you do for a living?" (He could have done anything in the world after all.) He said, 'Oh. I am a doctor. I own a chain of skin care clinics and I consult for twenty more.' (There is *The Law of Attraction* kicking in.) So I said, "I have this lady I would really like you to meet. Would you mind if I brought her to the meeting with me?" He said, 'I don't mind.' I asked him his name, it was Dr. Fei-pi Liu and we have become great friends.

About ten minutes later, she circled around and found me sitting in the parking lot. I said, "Don't worry. I have it all figured out. Next week we are going to meet with a doctor who owns his own chain of skin care clinics and consults for twenty more." She said, 'Wow! How did you do that?' I said, "I don't ask."

The following Wednesday we all sat down. She presented her product line. He purchased the goods. I then shared our product with him. He bought it as well. Then I said, "Do you look at passive and residual income streams?" He said, 'Residual income? Talk to me.' I then proceeded to share with him our business opportunity. At which time he said, 'Sign me up.'

Just over a month later, he reached the top level of our company. He now has over 800 people on his team and is about to earn the $100,000 ring with our company.

Now at this point some of you would say, 'Now, Gus, that is just plain lucky!' The answer is: that is absolutely not true. I say, ***"Luck is a loser's excuse for a winner's success."*** All those little things I did, which did not seem to make any difference, in fact, made all the difference in the world. Instead of me sitting at home, watching TV, doing nothing, I was out in the universe, being active. ***"Activity will beat inactivity any day of the week."***

Here are the morals to this story:
1. Do not put magnetic signs on the sides of your car. *I want everyone calling me*!
2. Don't help anybody. Then they will all come to me for help.

Seriously:
3. You all have the ability to help.
4. You don't have to be someone super special in order to be able to help someone out.
5. In all these little situations, was I ever planning on there being the payoff in the end? Could I have ever even seen it coming? No. I was not even looking for it.

6. I have helped people a countless number of times not ever looking for a payoff. Nevertheless, every time I have been paid back 10-fold or more.

7. We are all on ONE team, in business and in life; we should all help each other, every chance we get.

The Suit

No matter where you are or what you do, it is crucial to always be acting in a manner, which sets a good example for others to follow. You never know who is watching. Too often celebrities and sports figures forget they are (unwittingly if nothing else) role models. In most business and especially the network marketing industry, this is incredibly important because everything you do will duplicate through your organization, positive or negative. This next story illustrates how acting with awareness to those around you can have a far greater impact than you can imagine.

One evening I was at my business overview with a small crew of individuals who help me set up for these events. This particular evening one of the men came into the room to help us set up, but he was dressed very unprofessionally. I approached him and politely informed him if he was going to attend these events he needed to dress more professionally, in other words 'to dress for success.' His response to me was, 'Well. I'm not a millionaire like you. I cannot afford a suit like that.' The message he was giving me was, you can afford to wear expensive clothes, and I can't. So I asked, "If you could afford a suit like this would you wear a suit like this?" He said, 'Sure I would!' I grabbed my suit and felt the material as I said, "Really? This is a pretty nice suit. Do you like how it feels?" He felt the suit and said, 'yes.' Do you like this suit?" He agreed he did. I said, "Great! I want to see you in a suit like this suit next week." To which he again replied, 'I can't afford that suit.' And I said, "Well sure you can. It is $75 at Wal-Mart and the tie is from the 99 Cent Store." He looked at me with a stunned look on his face, but the next week he showed up wearing a suit, a tie, and looking very sharp. Every event after, he was always dressed very professionally.

There is a saying goes like this, *'Nothing succeeds like the appearance of success.'* However, there is nothing, which says the appearance of success must be expensive. Now if I had been wearing an $800 designer suit that week, what would I have told the guy at my meeting? I used to wear designer suits all the time; I don't do it anymore because the average person can't do it. As a leader, you must conscientiously set an example others can follow. If as a leader, you do things too out of the reach of the average person, they often will see it as an excuse for why they cannot be successful. As leaders, it is our responsibility to show people every reason why they can succeed.

"Setting an example for people is important. Setting an example which people can emulate is even better!"

-Gus Searcy

Chapter 12

Buffalo 1 – Jeep 0

Everyone has an addiction of one kind or another. My addiction is my cell phone. I suffer from it, and I admit it openly and freely. The moment they have cell phone implants available I will be the first one in line to get one. On average I use anywhere from 10,000 to 15,000 minutes per month. For me, having an unlimited plan is a very big deal.

One year, while on vacation with my family in Yellowstone National Park the strangest thing happened to me. The best part is I am here today to tell you about it. After you hear this story, I hope you remember sometimes the best thing you can do is nothing and just relax. Tensing up can be very dangerous, and even deadly.

In Yellowstone National Park, there is no cell phone service. One night while we were at a campsite, I happened to mention there was no cell phone service and the "withdrawals" I was having. The woman next to me leaned over and said to me, 'Well, you know there is this one place. If you go down the road about five miles outside the camp, then turn down the dead-end road, go up to the top of the hill, get out of your car, hold on to the antenna, lean to the left and put one foot in the air you will be able to get reception.' I quickly replied, "I'm there!"

So I told my family, "I'm going to go get cell service." Since they knew about my phone addiction, they did not expect me back anytime soon.

Off I went into the middle of nowhere in search of cell service. I reached the dead-end road in the middle of nowhere and jumped out of my car. I grabbed the antenna, leaned to the left and sure enough, I had reception. I made all my necessary calls, checked in on everything. Everything was great. I was done with my calls much quicker than I had anticipated, so I headed back to our campsite.

There was a new moon that night so it was pitch black outside. As I said I was in the middle of nowhere in my 1996 Jeep Grand Cherokee. Now I love my Jeep, almost more than life itself, but the head lighting system on that year was absolutely terrible, especially the brights (note: this has been rectified in newer models).

I was driving along, amazingly, under the speed limit, because it was so dark. Now mind you, it was quite unusual for me to be driving under the speed limit, especially 10 miles under the speed limit. Then to my complete surprise, I saw a buffalo standing right in the middle of the road. The buffalo's fur was a very dark brown, the car lights sucked right into its coat and there was no reflection from my headlights, whatsoever. So by the time I saw the buffalo I was almost on top of it.

Just in the nick of time, I yanked my wheel to the right as hard as I could. Then I looked and noticed I was headed straight for a cliff, so I quickly yanked my wheel back to the left. Now, since I was in an SUV I was sure I was going to flip the Jeep. (I had seen all of the public service warnings about how easily SUVs can flip.) But as sure footed as a cat the car stayed firm on the ground and I had just enough time to think, "Wow! I made it!" Then boom, a second buffalo... I hit the second buffalo and off the cliff I went.

At this point, everything went into slow motion. Most people do not know or understand how slow motion happens in those precise moments. Under most circumstances, your brain processes what is happening around you at the speed of sound (approximately 200 mp/hour). In emergency situations, once your adrenalin kicks in, your brain begins to process at almost the speed of light (186,000 mp/sec), which allows you to process an extensively greater amount of information in a very brief time which causes the feeling of "slow motion."

So at this point, to my knowledge, I was falling off a cliff and thought I was surely going to die. How could I not die? We have all seen plenty of cartoons and movies where the car goes off the cliff. Every time, without fail, the car blows up and the person dies. I instantly remembered those cartoons and movies and was sure this was to be my fate as well.

Then a moment later, I realized I was not falling. In fact I was rolling. It turned out, what I had seen, as a cliff in the dark was more of a small hill. Halfway through the first roll I was upside-down. Everything around me was floating. It was pitch black dark, since my headlights had blown out when I hit the buffalo. Then the "positive moment," I thought, "Wow! These seatbelts work really well. This is kind of like the Space Mountain ride at Disneyland. Not bad." I became completely relaxed and decided to just go with it and enjoy the ride.

I rolled all the way down the hill. I hit the bottom. The front end of my Jeep was gone. The roof was crushed. It rolled one more time and landed square on all four tires.

I was certain I was going to be surrounded by a herd of buffalo. The rangers had warned us repeatedly, 'Stay away from the buffalo during mating season.' And at this point I was thinking to myself, not only am I in trouble because it is mating season, but there is going to be one buffalo for sure who is really upset with me.

I decided to try the gas pedal, and it worked. As quickly as I could, I tried to figure out which way was up, (after what I had just been through, it was a bit like "Pin the Tail on the Donkey") and which way was back toward the campsite. I have a "thing" about flashlights. I have always told my children from the time they were little: "Flashlights are for emergencies!" In that moment, my flashlight obsession paid off. I have a flashlight everywhere, *just in case*. In this case, I could reach my ridiculously expensive (but powerful) little Starfire flashlight I had stashed in my Jeep. I pointed the flashlight in the direction I thought the campsite was, hit the on button and it lit up like the sun. Sure enough, I could see where I was. I threw the Jeep into 4-wheel drive and drove back up the hill I had just rolled down.

Sure enough, I made it all the way to the top and to the ranger's station. The rangers came out, saw the Jeep, saw me, and wanted to call an ambulance to take me away. I assured them I was fine. They asked me to stay there while they sent a couple of rangers out to the scene. After measuring the skid marks they verified I had not been speeding. Also from evaluating me the rangers could see I had not been drinking, so there was no penalty or citation issued. Then the ranger said, 'By the way, the buffalo is just fine.'

Crazy enough as it was, the Jeep still ran and we were on vacation with no other vehicle so we drove it around. Over the next few days, all the rangers came by to visit and see the Jeep. It was so unbelievable to them no one, human or beast, had died. In this case, both the animal and the individual were uninjured, and it was astonishing.

The story spread through the park and shortly the rangers were not the only ones coming by to see if it was true. Finally, after a couple days of getting the same questions over and over again, we put signs in the windows answering all the questions people kept asking. On the top of the page, it said: 'Buffalo – 1 Jeep – 0.' Then below we listed the following facts: 'Yes. This is the Jeep which hit the buffalo.' 'Yes. The buffalo is fine.' It was such frenzy; people were even asking if they could take pictures. At one point, a Japanese tourist off one of those tour buses asked me to put my arm around his wife so he could take a picture of us. It was quite the story and from it, I came away with two new major thoughts.

* * * *

First: Orison Swett Marden said, *"Every experience in life, everything with which we have come in contact in life, is a chisel which has been cutting away at our life statue, molding, modifying, and shaping it. We are part of all we have met. Everything we have seen, heard, felt, or thought has had its hand in molding us, shaping us."*

For me it was the knowledge that my instant decision to 'go with the moment' as crazy as it seemed, was the correct one. Therefore, it will be easier to trust my decisions in the future based on this experience.

And Second: If you are going to go off a cliff, it is best to do it in a Jeep Grand Cherokee!

Chapter 13

The Search For The Last First Kiss!

After the drama of my divorce finally simmered down, I had decided it was time to move forward. I was looking for my "last first kiss." To my dismay, this dating thing turned out to be right up there with root canals. Having been married for 30 years, dating was something I was no longer good at. I have met some wonderful women along the way. From a beauty queen and an actress to a stripper, a porn star, and even a princess, I have seen it all. Some were not right for me, while for others I was not right for them. Through those trials and tribulations, I learned a few harsh truths along the way. I hope, because of my sharing, you may not have to learn these hard lessons the way I did.

1) This was not a class I signed up for, but if I was going to have to get an "A" in it, a positive attitude and a sense of humor were definitely going to be required.

2) (And I know I am going to catch flack for this one) For <u>most</u> women, ***"The <u>thrill of the chase</u> is more important than the <u>quality of the catch</u>."*** As one man put it: *"I chased her until she caught me!"*

3) ***"It is not about "<u>finding</u>" the right person ... it's about "<u>being</u>" the right person."*** Many people have asked me "What do you mean by the statement, it is not about "finding" the right person, it's about "being" the right person. How did you get to this point? Being the right person and finding the right person go hand in hand don't they?"

Finding the right person for YOU makes it about you, and what <u>you</u> 'want.' 'Being' the right person is about being what the other person needs. When you make it about giving to them and being what they need, instead of getting from them what you want, it changes your dynamic and perspective from self-gratification to fulfillment of someone else.

If they are willing to reciprocate and be the right person for you, then it becomes a two way loving and giving relationship. The old adage "It is better to give then to receive" takes on a deeper meaning when applied here. Here are some of my dating highlights:

The Dates

1) **Who was that in the picture?** - About half of the women I met did not look anything like their picture. Not even as a relative!

2) **"Let's get married."** - We went on our first date and I sat across the table from her. She was a nurse, 10 years on the job (That should show she had stability, right?). I walked her to her car and gave her a "social" hug good-bye. The next day I received a call from her, informing me we had to get married. She was serious. She said I was 'The One.'

OK, I am willing to go as fast as a woman wants (Note: not looking for quick sex or one-night stands) but if we hit it off, I always let the woman decide the pace (as you will see next). So FAST is good, but there is a "natural" progression to it. Example: Meet … talk … eat … hold hands … kiss … really kiss … cuddle … make love … get married. You cannot skip steps!

3) **46 Year Old Virgin** – She was saving herself for her future husband to have kids with him (did I mention 46 years old?) enough said.

4) **Too Slow** – She was so afraid of getting hurt she wanted to go slow (as I said the woman sets the pace). After nine official dates, still no kissing, just starting to hold hands. I am patient, but does anyone else see a problem here? She said I am the best she has ever met (go figure).

5) **Tit for Tat** - Our first meeting, I was on time; she was 15 minutes late. Ok this is Southern California – traffic can be a problem. I was gracious about it, and the date went well. It went so well, we agreed to meet the next day. She was very pretty and seemed nice. In fact, I wondered why she was still single (It didn't take long to figure this one out). On that day, I was running late due to an accident on the freeway. I called her to let her know and said I would be there in five minutes. I called her three minutes later to tell her I was two minutes away. She asked me if I knew how to get home from where I was. I said "yes." She said, 'Good. Go home.' She had left because she did not like to be kept waiting.

6) **"What kind of S**T car is this?"** – I was running around town ... bank, etc. I was in my 1996 Jeep Grand Cherokee, which gets pulled behind my motor home and is washed when God washes it (which is not often in Southern California). In the world in which I operate this Jeep (as is) is legendary and has great significance to me. On this day, while I was out running errands, I received a call from one of the women from a dating website I was on. As luck would have it, I was only four miles away, so I agreed to meet her for coffee. She was out front when I arrived, and when she saw me she walked up to the jeep and said, 'What kind of S@#T car is this?!' I asked, "Does it matter?" And she said, 'Yes, of course! It tells me you are a dirty person and not very successful. If you were, you wouldn't be driving this S#@T car.' She was so upset she refused to even sit down with me to

have coffee. At, which point, I said: "Well too bad you feel that way". I then said, "For the record, I have a $40,000 sports car, a $250,000 dollar motor home, and a three million dollar house. All of which now you will never see." And I left. I am so glad I was in my Jeep that day!

7) **The "User"** - They have no interest in you other than what you can spend on them. While I have many examples I could give you, this is probably the best one to drive the point home.

I met a woman from a dating site and on our first meeting; we had mutually decided to lunch together. To be in the "spirit" of dating traditions, I told her she could pick the restaurant and I would pay. (I am still old school on this topic, but it may change.) Anyway, we met, and sat down to order. After she ordered her lunch, she proceeded to order another meal to go. I looked at her a bit bewildered. Then she said, 'Oh, thank you. This is for dinner so I won't have to cook later.' When the bill came, she never offered to pay for the to-go order. I never saw or tried to hear from her again.

Unfortunately, there are many of the "user" types out there.

8) **I guess I'm not as ready as I thought for a relationship** - (I ran in to this one the second most). They pique your interest. They start to know you and you them, and then they decide they are not ready for a

new relationship. This is confusing to me, because some part of them drove themselves to be on a dating website and go through all of the effort to set it up, look through names, and start corresponding with men. Yet when they find one who just might be everything they want, they shut down.   They make statements like, 'I am overwhelmed.' or 'I guess I'm just not ready.'

The key here is not to withdraw but to continue forward. It does not mean, "Jump into bed," but it does mean, "Jump into Life!" People spend a lot of time talking about "the quality of life." And having "quality time." Here is my spin on these statements, ***"The Quality of Life depends upon the Quality of Time invested in it!"*** I have had many   'If only I'd met you at a different time.' Here is what I tell them:

"What if, is what you are left with after Why not, is gone."   **- Gus Searcy**

9) **The Other Guy -** (*I received this one the most*). Here are two examples. Example one: You ask if they are over their other relationship. One week later, after you asked the question, they get married to "the other guy!" Example two: You have been texting and on the phone with them for a couple of months, so you drive 1600 miles to meet them. They are wonderful, just what you hoped for. However, distance is an issue. You spend a week with them and their kids. Their kids fall in love with you, and you fall in love with them, only to find out she really is not over the other guy. Even before you

leave the house, they are back on the phone together and you drive 1600 miles back home with your heart in your throat.

10) **Rules, Rules, Rules!** - These are women that have rules for everything. Rules for who they will and will not date, when they will date, how the man MUST act on the date, what can and cannot be done on any particular date. Heck, they even have rules for how you ... well, you get the idea. They are so busy with their rules they miss the bigger picture.

The first "rule" of life is there are no rules! It is only what people agree to. Rules and ground rules are fine but both parties need to know what those rules are from the beginning, as opposed to waiting for the man to stumble upon or against them. They leave no room for flexibility. There are exceptions to every rule and rules are made to be broken.

11) **The Combatant** – This is a most unusual category, to say the least. I have had several run-ins with them. The first time I encountered one I was caught off guard by the experience. From the very first date, they take offense to, or challenge most everything I say. They put me down or argue about the way I talk, the way I dress, even the color of my car. They put down my work and my philosophies of life. The strangest thing of all is after the date, a few days later, I hear from them wanting to know, 'When are we going out again?' I guess if you are a masochist, it is good to know your perfect match is waiting out there!

12) **The Green-Eyed Monster** – This is the stuff Hollywood scripts are made of. For those not familiar with the term "Green-Eyed Monster", it refers to someone who is jealous. One of the first to coin the phrase was William Shakespeare.

Iago:
O,   beware,   my   lord,   of   jealousy;
It is the green-eyed monster which doth mock the meat it feeds on;

A little possessiveness is OK, even desirable (it's nice to know you are valued), but jealousy is another world. My Green Eyed Monster was from another solar system! Here is how it went…

We first met; we hit it off right away. In fact, I was surprised how well we got along. For the first two weeks, it was great; then her 'green eyes' started to show. It started with her questioning me as to where I was going and who I was seeing. Then it progressed to she would go with me so she would not worry about me. It went steadily downhill from there. She would become upset every time a female talked to me. When we were in the supermarket, I would be admonished every time she (not me) saw a woman she thought was pretty. Believe it or not, it got worse. How much worse, you say? How about this: I live in one of the most automated homes in the world. The house is voice controlled and has a personality. The house's name is Angela, and when I speak to her, she answers me in a human perfect female voice complete with a French accent. She was even jealous of her! Finale score: Jealousy 1 – Love 0

13) **8 minutes is too long** – Aside from online dating I have tried my hand at other forms in initial contacts with women, and 8 Minute Speed Dating was one of them. For those of you who are not familiar with this form of dating, it goes something like this: A group of men and women meet at a restaurant and the women are each seated at a small table. They have a nametag with their first name and a number on it. The men also have a nametag with their first name and a number. A bell is rung and each man approaches a table and sits down for an 8-minute date with the woman seated at the table. After eight minutes, the bell rings again and the man gets up and proceeds to the next table. Each person, both men and women, have with them the equivalent of a dance card to keep notes on each date. At the end of the night, they all go home, log in to the dating site, and input the name and number of each person they would like to see again. If the numbers match, they receive the necessary information to contact the other person. Let me say up front it was an enjoyable experience, and I am sure quite a viable avenue for some people to pursue.

Even though each date is only eight minutes long, sometimes that is seven minutes too much. As an example, I submit the following: The bell rang and I approached the table of a woman and had a seat. She said, 'Hello' and I responded with "Hi, What do you like to do?" (Remember we only have eight minutes here.) She said, 'I like to tell jokes.' (Note the plural of the word "joke"). I said, "Great, tell me one." She had a puzzled look on her face and after stuttering a bit said, 'I only know one.' I thought, ok maybe she had misunderstood the question or I had misunderstood the answer. Anyway, I had her tell me the joke, which was ok but poorly told. So just to clarify my thinking I said to her, "When I sat down you said you like to tell jokes, yet you only know one joke," She said, 'Yes, I do like to tell jokes.' The next seven minutes seemed to last forever.

14) **The Analyst - Suffers from Analysis Paralysis -** This kind of woman analyzes every aspect of words, sentences, paragraphs to the point she never talks to or meets the guy she is trying to get to know. It all becomes about assumptions and analysis of words in a text or email, rather than human interactions and observations. Important things such as voice tones, body language, and physical chemistry are bypassed, so much so in the end, nothing happens and they never meet. Here is one case:

We met online, traded messages on the dating site a few times and then switched to emails (tons of them) and hours of chatting online. She even categorized the many things we had in common. And I quote:
'There are too many similarities. It's pretty scary. I would be AMAZED if there's not an earth shattering connection between us.

1. We both have sugar gliders & love them (most people do not even know what they are).

2. We both like to travel.

3. My female Jack Russell sleeps on my bed every night & you said your dog sleeps on your bed also and it's a male Jack Russell!

4. We both love animals in general.

5. HALO-The song Halo was on both our dating profiles and what we are both looking for.

6. We are both looking for 'the one,' our 'last first kiss'.

7. We both hate the dating game.

8. Both have a Carmel obsession & are interested in exploring the possibilities

9. Mirrors everywhere (even the ceiling!).

10. Items 10 through 17 cannot be discussed for this book is rated PG.

18. We both had enough respect for the relationships we were in to possibly let true love slip by so as not to hurt the other person.

Unfortunately, because a situation did come up, I need it completely resolved before I can meet or talk on the phone'.

Despite the fact her heart felt we were connecting, her mind refused to accept it. She was convinced I was lying because it all sounded too good to be true (now remember this is only to have a first meeting, not a true date!) Here is how she put it:

'My problem is my gut is still telling me what my heart and brain don't want to hear and I will know when I meet you if my gut is right. So a meet and greet is going to be either really good or REALLY bad. If my gut is right & you've been lying, it won't matter what my heart thinks anymore. That's what makes it SO scary because as far as things in common and weird coincidence (We even have the same kind of dog)! I can't see where it could go wrong.'

No action was taken. We never did meet.

This reminds me of a story I heard about some birds sitting on a wire. ***"If there are three birds sitting on a wire and one decides to fly away, how many are left?"*** "Two?" You may say. The answer is three! You see the one bird, which decided to fly away is still there because though it <u>decided</u> to fly away it never took action. To decide is not enough, action must be taken for something to happen.

15) **The Sad and Wounded**-Maybe it is due to the age group I am dating in or maybe just the times we now live in, but there are many, many unhappy and jaded people out there. One wonderful woman in particular was feeling trapped in an unhappy relationship and many, many years of being tortured about giving her son up for adoption forty some years before. Her son had recently found her, and they were both going through a lot of pain and hurt.

Because she knew I wrote poems, she asked me to write her one on adoption. She told me cynically I would not understand how she felt. I thought about it and wanted to try to show her the positive side of her decision. So I wrote the poem and presented it to her. The poem surprised and admittedly impressed her beyond her expectations. This is what I wrote for her:

Adoption

Over many years and with social changes, women raised their voice.
So when they face the unexpected, they then would have a choice.

When you're not ready to have a child, it's hard to know or guess,
Not to have them, or to have one, a No's easier than a Yes!

But to have a child, is quite a job, it requires money, time, and care,
To try to keep them without these, to the baby is not fair.

So out of love and for what's best, the Mother may decide,
To find her child a better home and quickly step aside.

Of all the choices women have, this is the hardest one,
Because though the baby now is gone, her love is never done.

Throughout her life with tortured tears, and her baby not in sight,
She'll lie awake on sleepless nights, wondering if she'd done what's right.

But in her time of stress of strife, she chose the hardest option,
Not to end the life, but instead, give her baby for adoption.

* * * * *

So, with respect to my dating experiences you might be saying to yourself, 'OK so where is the positive in all of this?' Actually, there are several positives here and a big one as you will see in a moment. Just based on the small sample of my experiences you read above, the first is maintaining a positive attitude toward the process. It would be very easy to become jaded, disheartened, quit trying and just wait for "it" to happen.

Second, is the understanding you can just sit back and let fate decide your outcome. However, it is better to understand through the positive way of thinking you have a more positive option. *"Fate is an opportunity for new choices where none existed before!"* In other words as someone once said, you can 'ride the bus' or 'drive the bus.' If you ride the bus, you go where the bus driver is going and at the speed, it is going. If you drive the bus, however, you decide the speed and direction and you are participating in your own rescue!

Despite approaching some 2,760 dating prospects (mostly on-line), and 897 "dates," I continuously chose the positive option. Had these women done the same, many of our encounters may have ended quite differently. Nonetheless, I chose to remain un-jaded and optimistic. If I truly am to find my "Last First Kiss," I must not let any of the less-than-pleasant experiences of my past affect my future. I knew it would not be long in the future before I would walk into a room and for the first time look into the eyes of the woman who will become the love for the rest of my life, and it would all have been worthwhile.

It was Abraham Lincoln who said: *"The best thing about the future is it comes one day at a time!"*

Now some of you may say, 'how could you know this with just a first look?' As I said, I am searching for "the one" and the moment I see her I will know. *She* may not, but I will. When I was 19, I was in college and I walked into a party. There were 35 girls from the local sorority there. I looked across the room and saw one girl in particular. She looked back at me, and we were together for seven years... A while after the relationship had ended; I went to a restaurant with a co-worker to get lunch. The waitress walked up to the table and asked 'may I help you?' When she walked away, I turned to the co-worker and said, "That is who I am going to marry." Even though it took one year to get brave enough to ask her out, we were together 30 years. There is a book called "Blink" by Malcolm Gladwell which explains what I am doing is way more than just looking at the physical, AKA "Lust at first sight." It is an instant, multifaceted analysis based upon parameters such as pheromones, instinct, and personal preferences all happen within seconds after I meet someone and look into her eyes.

And then it happened... One day I was contacted from the dating web site by a woman who wanted to meet me, (a psychic no less!) so I agreed. When we met, she did not look anything like her picture or physical description. I instantly knew she was not someone I was interested in. However, since I always try to maintain a positive attitude about things, I decided to have the date anyway. I was across the street when I first saw her and could have easily left there and then. Despite my lack of interest in her as a future partner, I stayed with her and bought us dinner. I was polite and later found out several of her first dates excused themselves to the bathroom and never came back or stuck her with the bill and left. Toward the end of dinner she said, 'I feel I am not the one you are looking for' (Well she IS a psychic after all!) I said no she was not, but when I see her, I will know.

After she inquired about my business and understanding what I did, she went on talking about it and said she had a friend, whom could use my help. I agreed to meet with her and her friend in the next few days. The "psychic" then tentatively set up a meeting with the woman who needed help. On the appointed day, I had not heard from the "psychic" to confirm the meeting. In addition, she had not returned any of my calls all day long. It would have been very easy not to show up at this point because it was only an unconfirmed *tentative* appointment, but I had promised to come so I went anyway. A positive choice I am most thankful for.

There is a saying: *"Successful people do what unsuccessful people are unwilling to do."*

As I walked up to the table I noticed three women sitting there, not the two I was expecting. As I sat down at the table I was introduced by the psychic to the one I was supposed to help and then to a friend of the Psychic who she had also invited to come along (who I later found out the psychic had specifically invited to come meet me). As I was introduced to her, I looked into the eyes of the woman as she sat there. My heart started beating harder, alarms went off in my head, and I had the feeling of being on the downhill slope of a rollercoaster. I had just "Blinked." Her name is Terry, and we are together to this day!*

What if my attitude had been the same as those other men's had been? In a strange way, I should thank them for having a negative attitude. Because if they had not, I would not now be looking into the eyes, of My Last First Kiss!

*Update: As of the publishing of this book, we are engaged to be married!

Chapter 14

Odds and Ends

At this point, I hope you have enjoyed this book and my stories. The following chapter is a compilation of a few extra stories, which did not get their own chapter and later, a few more side notes and side stories about some of the previous chapters. Enjoy.

The Grandfather Clock

We May Have Time, But There
Is No Such Thing As Someday.

At one time in my life, I was an outside sales representative working in the copier industry. One day, around lunchtime, I was in Lakewood, California, which was part of my territory. I decided to take my lunch break at the Lakewood Shopping Center. When I arrived there, Snow's Clock Shop caught my eye. You see, I have a quirk. Well, most people do have a quirk of some kind. Some people hoard junk or newspaper in their homes. Some people are superstitious and some people walk around the house with only one sock on. For example, my son Brandon, from the moment he could walk to today at 18 years old, he can still be seen walking around the house with only one sock on. In my case, I need things that **move, whirr, click, or blink**. In fact, in every single room of my house I have something, which whirrs, moves, clicks, or blinks. I have this down to such an obsession, I even have something in the dining room, which would not typically have something of that nature in it. In my dining room, I have indoor windless wind chimes. Therefore, it was no surprise the clock shop caught my eye while I was out on my lunch break. I decided to walk in. Just before I entered the store a silver-haired couple was just in front of me, and I held the door open for them.

As we strolled through the store admiring all the beautiful clocks, I was never far away from this endearing little couple. As they approached one particular large grandfather clock, the couple admired it for a few minutes. Then the woman looked at her husband and said, 'Honey this is absolutely a beautiful clock. Don't you agree?' He looked at her and said, 'Yes. It is very beautiful.' She then said, 'I'd like to have a clock like that someday.' He replied, 'You know what, Honey?

Someday perhaps we will.' They admired the clock for a few more moments and then moved on.

After they left the store, I stood watching them as they walked away. I looked at the clock they had been admiring and thought to myself, "When is someday?" As old, as they were it did not seem as though they had very many 'somedays' left.

There is a famous saying, which goes like this, *"Procrastination is the grave in which opportunity is buried." (Author Unknown)*

As I looked at the clock, I asked the owner how much it was. When he told me I felt it was a pretty expensive clock, so I decided to rephrase my question, "How much would the clock cost per month?" After he answered the question, I realized, <u>without going into debt</u>, if I was willing to give up lunch for one year, I could have the clock <u>that</u> day, and not 'someday.'

I did give up lunch for one year, and to this day, I still admire the grandfather clock in my home. I have enjoyed it for a countless number of 'somedays.'

"To be always intending to live a new life, but never find time to set about it-this is as if a man should put off eating and drinking from one day to another till he be starved and destroyed." - Sir Walter Scott

Life Size Amanda

As parents, we all try to do the best thing for our kids. We want to make sure they grow up to be good citizens and good people. As a parent, you always look for the moment when you can rest assured and know your child will be a great person.

I have four children: Amanda, Hilliary, Brandon and Sean, all of whom are wonderful. Each one of them is unique and different in their own way. My oldest one is Amanda. Being the oldest she was the first one through the system, if you will. I had the privilege of watching her go through all the phases and there was one very specific and defining moment when I knew she was going to be a good person.

When Amanda was seven years old, she received a Life-Size Barbie from Santa Claus for Christmas. She was absolutely in love with her toy. Her little sister, Hilliary, who is two and a half years younger than Amanda is, also loved that Life-Size Barbie. All year long, the Barbie was played with continually.

Next Christmas came and all Hilliary was talking about was how much she wanted her own Life-Size Barbie. To this request Amanda kept saying, 'Don't worry. You have been a good girl this year. Santa will bring you one.' Around Christmas time, my wife and I started freaking out because they were no longer making Life-Size Barbie's. You couldn't get them anywhere. We did not know what we were going to do. We even attempted to guide Hilliary's attention to other things, other toys, other gifts, but nothing could compete. All she wanted was the Barbie. Of course, Amanda was not helping at all because she kept reassuring Hilliary not to worry, Santa would bring her one. How were we supposed to argue with that?

We were able to find Life-Size Barbie clothes, so we bought some of those and wrapped them up. Nevertheless, when Christmas Eve came, we felt pretty lousy. Moreover, the last thing Amanda told Hilliary before bedtime was, 'Don't worry. Santa Claus will make sure you get your Life-Size Barbie.'

Christmas morning came, and we all went downstairs together to open presents. To my wife's and my surprise, there was an extra present under the tree neither of us had seen or expected. As we noticed it, we both looked at each other with the questioning look, (Did you get something else?), and neither of us had. On the present it said, 'To: Hilliary, From: Santa.' She opened it, and it was a Life-Size Barbie.

Apparently, what had happened was Amanda had woken up early Christmas morning before everyone else, went out, and looked under the tree. When she realized, there was no Life-Size Barbie under the tree for Hilliary she went back to her room, cleaned up her own Life-Size Barbie, wrapped it in Christmas wrapping paper, and put in under the tree for her sister, Hilliary. (Remember: Amanda was eight.)

Most eight-year-olds would not have the level of awareness or concern for someone else, let alone have the forethought to do such a thing. That was the moment when I knew Amanda was going to be a wonderful adult.

Fast forward to today: At 22 years old, Amanda finished her second bachelor degree, and graduated as a nurse from Loma Linda University. She passed her board certification with a perfect score and became a registered nurse. Amanda is now 24 and married to a wonderful man named Rod. She is working as a full time nurse at Saint Mary's in Apple Valley. She has chosen a life path of helping others, and that generous heart of hers made itself known Christmas morning when she was eight years old.

The power of Amanda's positive choice kept the Christmas spirit alive in our home that year, which may not have otherwise been possible.

Food for Thought

There was a time in my life when I was traveling all over the world. Somewhere along the way, eating became very boring and unfulfilling for me. When I became aware of this boredom, I realized it was because no matter where I was in the world, be it China, be it Italy, I would always order only one of roughly five different meals. I only ordered hamburgers or other meals which were similar enough to what I was used to back home, despite the fact they never satisfied my taste buds the way the food from home did.

On one particular occasion, while I was in China, I was meeting with government officials regarding my voice recognition invention. I was meeting with about ten of their top engineers, programmers and people of that sort. Additionally, there was an interpreter there, because I was the only individual in the meeting who did not speak Chinese. We had been working for quite some time and then the lunch hour arrived.

One of the gentlemen said something to the interpreter, after which the interpreter asked me if I was hungry. I said, "Sure." He said blah blah blah back to them. They said blah blah blah back to him, and then he asked me what I would like to eat. I said, "Anything is fine." The interpreter relayed my response back to the gentleman who then began to laugh. I asked why they were laughing. Then he said, 'Well, you said 'anything'.' I then told the interpreter I was going to look directly at the gentlemen, not at him, and I wanted him to interpret to the gentlemen exactly what I was going to say. I then turned to the gentlemen and said, "I will eat anything you do, as long as one of you eats it in front of me first." The interpreter said blah blah blah to them. At which point they all started chatting amongst themselves and within moments, they all broke out in laughter. Then we all went out for a *Fear Factor* 'food challenge', Chinese style.

One of the men told me that Chinese philosophy is to eat anything whose 'back is to the sun'. In other words, anything, which moves: animal, fish or insect, it does not matter. In fact, some of the things were so "unusual" the gentlemen would draw straws amongst themselves to see who would have to eat it in front of me so I would in turn eat it as well. Needless to say, at the end of it all they were very impressed because I did in fact eat everything they ate. To this day some of the things I ate with those gentlemen still haunt me.

However, from the experience I came away with a new outlook on things, especially eating. A few days later when I went to dinner, the waiter asked me what I would like. I told him, "Oh, just bring me anything." Since then I have acquired a more refined approach. Now, whenever I go out to dinner with friends I am always the last to order and I say the following to the server, "Whatever I am going to have cannot be something anyone else at the table has already ordered. It cannot be a special of the day. It doesn't even have to be something from the menu. But whatever it is, I do not want to know what it is until you set it in front of me. No questions whatsoever."

This has turned out to be quite intriguing for the servers. I have actually had food paraded around the restaurant. I have had new menu items, which restaurants were considering, tried out on me. I have had chefs prepare something especially for me. Moreover, I can honestly say not one time have I ever been disappointed.

So from the food challenge experience I gained a very positive experience and outlook by being able to try almost everything.

Now the reality is there are three things I really do not like. I am not fond of eggplant. I don't like lima beans, but I have never seen them in a restaurant. And I do not eat veal, out of social protest. Thus far, those have not been issues in my adventures of culinary exploration.

Servers usually enjoy this experience as well. They are usually quite intrigued, and they always smile. The people at my table are also pretty amazed and everyone is excited to see what I will be served to eat. All and all this provides a positive experience for all parties involved, especially me.

The willingness to be adventurous and take a risk most people would not usually take has yielded me delicious rewards time and time again.

The Abacus

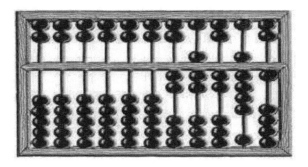

Since we are on the topic of travel, here is a story, which has an unexpected twist. Quite frequently, during times of travel, one faces many opportunities of positive or negative choices. Too often tourists take on a sense of entitlement as opposed to adopting more principles of respect and appreciation for the places and cultures in which they are visiting. I have always tried to make a habit of respecting and adopting the culture of the people and places I visit, as much as I can. The following story demonstrates the wonderful reward, which came when I made the positive choice to study the practice of another culture.

Throughout my world travels I have found it is always important, when I go to another country, to try to acclimate to their language and their customs. By doing this, I am better accepted and more people will go out of their way to help me. Too many people think everyone should try to talk and cater to them because they are the tourists with the money in their pocket. The reality is the more you try to become like them, the more they will appreciate it and accept you.

I was all by myself, wandering the streets of China, the only Caucasian, during Christmas time. It was around 10:00 at night. The shops all stay open pretty late there, almost all night. I walked into this one clothing store and started looking around. Not too long after being in the shop, I spotted a sweater on the wall I thought would be a really nice present for someone.

I only knew a few words in Chinese. However, I knew enough to ask, "How much is it?" The cashier looked up at me then pulled a large abacus out from under the counter. (Back then they used abacuses to calculate totals, not calculators.) He proceeded to flip some of the beads on the abacus, and then he wrote down a number, his asking price for the sweater I was interested in. What he did not know was I also knew how to use an abacus.

In this part of the world you barter over the prices of goods sold. After he offered me a price for the sweater I then took the abacus, spun it around toward me then flipped the beads around to show a different number than his original asking price. Then I flipped it around back to facing him. The look on his face was pure shock. Now I am only guessing, but I think at this point he said something along the lines of this to the people in the store, 'Hey people, you have to come see this! This white guy knows how to use an abacus!' All of a sudden all the clerks and customers stopped what they were doing and came and circled around us.

Then he put in another set of numbers on the abacus and spun it back to face me, almost as if to say, 'Alright. Now let's see if you really know how this works, or if it was just a lucky coincidence.' So, I took the abacus and punched in the price I wanted to pay and spun it back around to him. This time the look on his face was one of astonishment. He looked up at me, then at all the people gathered round. Judging by their response, I am betting he said something along the lines of, 'Wow. He does know how to use an abacus.' We haggled for one more round, and then after I presented my price he bowed to acknowledge his acceptance.

As I was paying for the sweater, everyone was bowing and clapping. After the clerk rang me up, he bowed one more time. As he bowed, he handed me the abacus as a present to keep. To this day, that very abacus sits on the shelf in my family room.

Because I had taken the time, to not only learn their customs and language, but their tool as well, I was able to enjoy a truly unique and incredible experience. Without my positive choice, it would not have been quite as wonderful an experience.

It is impossible to predict the rewards you will reap all because you chose to go the extra mile.

Coins of the Realm

Sometimes people are so involved doing one thing it is hard for them to change what they are doing despite what is right or wrong, or what may be better.

There was a time in my life when I was doing quite a bit of traveling all around the world. When I was in Italy at the top of the Leaning Tower of Pisa I noticed everyone was taking out little knives and carving their names or initials in the walls to leave their mark. At first, I thought this was cool and I was going to do the same. Then I realized what they were all doing was simply defacing this incredible piece of history. This is when I decided I too would leave my presence, but I was going to do something different. I wrote the following poem to my children so they could one day travel the world and discover all the places I left my "presents" for them to find,

Coins Of The Realm

Throughout the years, I have traveled much,
And far from, you did roam.
But no matter where I spent the night,
My thoughts were still of home.

To pass the time, to keep the faith,
And show my thoughts were true,
To each place I've gone and slept,
I've hid a coin for you.

Throughout the world by plane and car,
To far and distant lands,
A quarter did accompany me
And was hidden by my hands.

Each one was placed with loving care,
In a place that's sure to last,
For when you go and look for them,
Much time may have gone past.
To mark the spot where treasures hid,
And so there's no mistake,
A camera too accompanied me,
And pictures I did take.

For you my children this was done,
So in the future, you would see,
The world of places I have been
And have good thoughts of me.

For I love you all, and when you're grown,
May you have a chance to take the helm,
And travel too as I have done,
And find, Coins Of The Realm.

This poem is in a book, which I have created for my children and contain treasure maps, directions, and photographs showing them exactly how to find all the coins I have hidden for them, all over the world. There are coins in The Parthenon in Greece, Ming's Tomb, The Great Wall of China, Stonehenge, The Statue of Liberty,

The Emperor's Palace in Japan, Malaysia, Singapore, and Blarney Castle in Ireland, just to name a few.

By making a more positive choice of action than my fellow travelers made, not only did I not deface these wonderful places, but also I ended up creating a legacy for my children. By not following the masses, you will usually end up with a better result. This was the case here.

Ski Boots

There is a prevailing attitude in the world today, businesses are bad and are 'money grubbing capitalist', with no heart. If this is the attitude you take with them, then this is the response you will most likely get in return. If people would only try the "Golden Rule" (do unto others as you would have others do unto you) first, then resort to other measures they might get better results. Here is one example.

In 1985, my wife and I bought each other ski boots for Christmas. Due to "life" getting in the way, we did not even get to try to use them for almost 14 years. This is of course long after any warranty on them had expired and the company had no obligation to do anything whatsoever. The company was **Nordica** and this is the letter I sent to them:

~~~~~~~~~~~~~~~~~~~~~~~~~~~~~~~~~~~~~

April 13, 1999

Dear sir/madam:

Several years ago, my wife and I bought each other ski boots for Christmas.

For her   Model # NL 350
For me Model #NS 770

Due to a back injury to myself and then several years of my wife being pregnant with our four children we NEVER were able to use them (not even once!).

We are finally planning our first ski trip. Yesterday we each tried on our boots to see if they would still fit. They each broke apart like a chocolate egg.

We bought these boots (which were very expensive to us!) because they were the best there was and we were told they would last a long time. We are very saddened by this turn of events.

We know it has been a long time ago, and there is no "legal" obligation on your part, but we will be glad to send them to you for inspection so you can see they have NEVER been used. We only tried on one boot each, so one is broken and the other is still intact.

We supported your company by buying your products because we believed them to be the best. We are now also preparing to buy our four children ski equipment.

Can you somehow help us out now?

Sincerely,

Gus Searcy

Only a couple of weeks passed and then I received a call from one of the vice presidents of the company to ask me some questions about the letter I had sent. He was very pleasant and understanding to our predicament. He said he could not make any promises but asked if I would be willing to mail them our boots. I said "yes" and off they went. A few weeks later, we received a package from Nordica with two brand new pairs of top of the line ski boots.

I am sure if I had started with a hard line attitude or a "you owe me" approach the outcome would not have been the same. Remember after 14 years, Nordica had no obligation to do anything. They could not have known years later, they would receive publicity for this event or they would benefit in any way. We need to remember, companies are made up of people with feelings and problems just like us. Moreover, if our attitude is positive about a problem, it will tend to give them a positive attitude toward us and our situation.

Needless to say, Nordica is the only brand I buy to this very day, and I recommend them whenever I get the chance.

The Blue Parrot Lounge

The Blue

P
a
r
r
o
t

Lounge

This particular story happened back during my magician days. For a short while, there was some extra time where I had a break between events. At this particular time, I was hired to do a magic show for a private party at a very high-end hotel in Costa Mesa, California called the South Coast Plaza Hotel. This hotel was located right across the street from South Coast Plaza Mall.

After my show, I walked around the hotel and spotted an empty room called 'The Blue Parrot Lounge.' The lounge was very nice, and I noticed it had a stage. I thought to myself "Wow, maybe I could do magic here." Instead of just thinking about it, I took action on the idea and approached the hotel's general manager about the possibility of me performing magic there.

They thought it would be a good idea. After some promoting, I began to perform magic shows at The Blue

Parrot Lounge. The deal was I would perform three nights a week, two shows per night and the last show would end at 9:00 p.m. Between the shows, I would walk around to the guests at the tables and perform 'Table Magic' for them.

After about a month of these shows, the management was not sure if they were going to continue to keep the show running. They were not sure how the customers really felt about the show. The general manager was debating whether or not it should just be cancelled. Of course, I hoped they would allow me to continue to perform. This particular venue was not just great for the guests and me, it was also great for the many guest magicians I would showcase.

One of the last few nights before the general manager was going to make his final decisions of whether or not to extend the show for a few more weeks; I had finished the evening show and was hanging out in the lounge. During this particular show there had been two very attractive young women flirting with me throughout the show. 9:00 p.m. came and went, and the evening show ended. I was enjoying myself with the young women who then offered to take me out for dinner and drinks. This sounded like fun to me!

As we were walking through the lounge to leave together, around 9:30 p.m. two businessmen entered the lounge, sat down at a table, and asked if there was another magic show that night? Now, keep in mind, I was already off the clock, I had a beautiful woman on each arm, and we were all on our way out for dinner and drinks.

In that particular moment, I could have easily and rightfully chosen to say, "I'm really sorry; the last show did end at 9:00. Please, feel free to come back tomorrow for our next show." I could then have followed by giving them a flyer with the schedule showing the hours of our weekly shows. There was no obligation on my part. I had fulfilled my two-show commitment for the evening, and two beautiful women were a much more enticing offer.

However, along my journey, I had learned a very powerful principle, which jumped out at me. I believe Napoleon Hill said it best. *"If success is what you want, you must make a habit of doing more than you are paid for."* I made the choice in that moment to stay and perform for the businessmen, as reluctant as I was, I bid the ladies farewell.

That evening I performed a 'Table Magic' show for the two men, which lasted about forty-five minutes. They were quite entertained and thanked me for the show. After the show, they left. I went home and did not think much more about it.

Two days later, the general manager of the hotel called me into his office to inform me of whether or not he was going to keep the show. He shared, although he had heard many good reviews about the show, there was one review in particular which heavily influenced his decision. He said what he heard had impressed him. He then went on to share with me about the night before he was going to make his final decision, his brother and his brother's client had come in to the Blue Parrot Lounge sometime after the 9:00 p.m. show had ended. His brother and his client knew they had missed the last show but thought they would stop in anyway. They had been so impressed by not only the magic show, but by my choice to go above and beyond the call of duty when I clearly had a more appealing offer to leave with those two beautiful women. He saw I was dedicated and loyal to the hotel and the show. His brother recommended he keep me on. Because of the positive choice and my commitment, the general manager decided to keep my show running for an additional three months.

"Demand the best from yourself; because others will demand the best of you ... Successful people don't simply give a project hard work. They give it their best work."   *-Win Borden*

"I say to you, chose wisely. Always do more than you are paid for, it will always pay off."

Chapter 15

Happily Ever After

I am often asked, what my opinion is, regarding the secret to life. Most people seem fascinated with the quest for this answer, yet to me it is the simplest of all life's questions. This secret to life is this simple...

Life.... L. I. F. E.... **LOVE INTENTLY FOREVER!** Love is the most powerful force in the universe. To some this may seem like a trite answer but in fact, it is really the only possible answer for true happiness.

My father taught me your own heaven or hell is what you create for you right here on earth. For the most part for me it has been quite heavenly! I am not saying there have not been bad or sad moments. We all have them, but rather it is how we fight through them, which can make all the difference. In every case (whether you believe it or not) you have a choice ALWAYS, yet I hear people say 'I have no choice' or 'I am out of options.' Unfortunately, if this is what you 'think', then you are right. However, if you believe even in the most difficult of situations there are options and positive ones to boot, you will also be right. If you keep doing the same things over and over again and expect different results, that's called insanity. As a friend of mine said, "our philosophies affect our attitudes, our attitudes affect our actions, and our actions affect our life." If you change your philosophies to positive ones', your life will change for the better, forever.

The pessimist complains about the wind. The optimist expects it to change. The leader adjusts the sails. -JC Maxwell

Each new day we awake, we are given the opportunity to change our lives for the positive. It is up to us to make the simple small choices as we go so we learn to live our life to the fullest. I believe positive affirmations are important. I have made this one part of my personal life philosophies and say it daily. It goes like this...

Today is the first day of the rest of my life. It is up to me to decide how I will spend it. It is my duty to myself to be all I can be, discover, and develop the talent that lies within me. I am in charge of my personal destiny. I will always make positive choices. Though I have fears, I will learn to face them and use them as stepping-stones to success. I know that if it is to be... it is up to me. I am unstoppable, I am special, and I will live my life to the fullest, not only today, but every day, no delays, no exceptions, no excuses. <u>I will succeed!</u>

I know there are many people out there, either you or someone you know who have faced a difficult situation and made the positive choice with remarkable results. I would like to hear those stories from you. I have set up a website where you can see some documentation on the stories you have read in this book and a place there where you can contact me with your personal stories where "**the power of positive choice**" made all the difference.

www.thecharm.info

Chapter Notes

<u>Chapter 1 Once Upon a Time</u>

Adoption

When I learned I had been adopted I did not know why. Some years later, I learned before Dotty died she had set up a trust for me. When she died my family on her side fought my father for me. To insure Dotty's wishes be honored my father had my mother (Hazel) adopt me. This way if anything were to happen to him, I would stay with my mother, which is what Dotty wanted.

Becky

As we began to write this book it occurred to me, when all of these stories went public, someone out there might attempt to disprove the stories. I even thought about creating a website (<u>www.thecharm.info</u>) where people could just go to see the recorded facts of each story. For most of the book, this did not concern me one bit. Chapter 1 was the only chapter I was not sure, how I could go about proving, should anyone ask.

After we began writing the book, I sent this very thought out to the universe. *How could I prove or document*

Chapter 1? As crazy as it may sound, this is just how my life works.

One day, not too far into the process of creating the book, I received a message on Facebook that said they knew where my long lost niece might be. I answered back and a few days later my phone rings:

Gus: Hello.
Caller: Is this Gus?
Gus: Yes.
Caller: Searcy?
Gus: Yes.
Caller: This is Becky!

Becky is my step-niece. When my biological mother (Dotty) had chosen Hazel to be my mother she was a widow. She had a son from her first marriage. His name is William Dunn. By the time my mother Hazel came into my life, William was already an adult and no longer living with his mother, so he and I never lived together while I was growing up.

William Dunn married and had three daughters, Becky, Beth and Barbra. As life happens, there came a time when William and his family needed to stay with us for a few months. The oldest daughter Becky and I were close in age, and for a short while, we lived together as brother and sister. Then one day they moved away and I never saw any of them again.

It had been over 45 years since I had seen, or heard from any of them, before Becky called that day. This was very exciting! First of all how wonderful, she is alive! Furthermore, my stepbrother, William Dunn is still alive! What's more, William remembered the story of Dotty and our mother Hazel and documented the validity of Chapter 1.

Chapter 3 $1.10 to Six Figure Stocks

NOTE: While I was working at Mc Donald's to earn money so I could play the stock market and worked my way up to earning $1.10 an hour. I did not start off making much money. All the while, my allowance was 10 cents per week.

Happy Cup

While working at McDonald's, my high school decided to put a time capsule in the ground with the intention of opening it some 50 or so years later. It was my idea to sign a McDonald's Happy Cup put a in the time capsule. I persuaded a couple of the other guys who worked there with me to sign it also. So currently, someday when the time capsule at Warren High School in Downey, California, is to be dug up, there will be a McDonald's Happy Cup with my signature on it.

Quick Change Artist

Remember, back then because we did not have cash registers, we calculated everything by hand, or in my case in my head. Being things were done by hand, it was easy to make a mistake. Criminals will always be there to profit from the loopholes. Working at McDonald's they would always warn us to be careful of Quick Change Artists. Quick Change Artists would bring a $20 bill to the cashier and ask if they could get change. After the cashier opened the register they would say, "Oh could I get two fives, I mean one ten and two fives" and so on and so on. By the time they are done you have actually given them more change than you owe them. People would actually make a living this way back then.

One day while I was at work, I had the opportunity to duel with a Quick Change Artist. Being as I was a magician, I knew how his game was played, and I also was extremely good at math. Once I realized he was a Quick Change Artist, I could not wait to play. As we were going along, I interrupted him and said, "No, no wait, let me give you two fives instead of a ten and three ones..." And by the time we were done, I had more money than he did.

About the Author

Mr. Gus Searcy came into this world in an unusual way and has since lived an unusual and varied life. At age 16, his parents signed over power of attorney to him as an adult so he could play the stock market. Once they realized he really knew what he was doing, the only way to buy and sell over the phone was to give him 'adult' status. By 17, he was earning a 6-figure income and has been doing it every year since... (He jokes that's only about 5 years now). By age 19, he became a landlord owning one of the most rented condominiums in Mammoth, California. At age 21, he became the youngest owner in the world of a 7-11 franchise. By age 24 he owned a world champion Frisbee catching dog, which made more money than some people make in a lifetime. By age 26, as a performing member of the Magic Castle in Hollywood, California, he became one of the highest paid magicians in the world. By age 28, he invented and perfected a new product and technology, which landed his invention in the Smithsonian in Washington D.C. where it resides today. His success in life, and his very life itself, was made from a series of positive choices most people would not have made. This book is about those choices and how the power of positive choice can change your life as well!

Bibliography

Schwartz David J,
The Magic of Thinking Big:
4/2/1987
 Fireside Books

Jeff Olson,
The Slight Edge:
11/25/2011
Success Media

Malcolm Gadwall,
Blink: The Power of Thinking Without Thinking:
January 11, 2005
Little, Brown and Company

Rhonda Byrne,
The Secret:
November 28, 2006
Atria Books/Beyond Words

Robert Kiyosaki
Rich Dad Poor Dad
April, 2000
Plata Publishing

Leigh Harline and Ned Washington,
When You Wish upon a Star:
1940, Bourne Co. Music Publishers